"A practical guide for every loving parent. What a great job the authors have done to make the seemingly complex job of being a parent a lot simpler."

~ Dr. Kevin Leman, Adlerian author of *The Birth Order Book*, and many other parenting best-sellers, host of Reality Talks.com

"*Positive Discipline in the Christian Home* is a combination of depth and practical simplicity. Based on philosophical, Biblical, and ethical principles, this book should be in every church library and every Christian family home."

~ Paul Faulkner, PhD, professor, Abilene Christian University; author of *Making Things Right When Things Go Wrong*

"I have been teaching parenting from the *Positive Discipline in the Christian Home* since its first publishing in 2001. I am delighted to see these wonderful tools connected to the Scriptures. Most of the families who attend my classes are young parents who desire to raise their children to love God and others and to learn how to apply the tools with kindness and firmness, a balance that is so imperative in creating a loving environment that exemplifies Biblical teaching. The parents express how the descriptive Biblical text and practical examples bring clarity and joy to their parenting."

~ Jan Morris, Certified Positive Discipline Lead Trainer and Parent Coach

"From the beginning, Judeo-Christian teachings have served as a guide to traditional family life and child rearing. Now the highly complementary principles and practical applications of Positive Discipline are intertwined with a firm foundation of faith to assist parents in raising moral children in today's turbulent, fast-paced society."

~ Linda E. Jessup, MPH, FNP, founder of the Parent Encouragement Program (PEP, Inc.), greater Washington, D.C.

"An exciting book! A must-read guide for parents who desire to bring true Christian teachings and principles into their child-rearing practices."

~ Reverend Peggy Goochey, minister with Children & Families, First United Methodist Church

"In a world inundated with clichéd self-help books and easy feel-good solutions to every challenge, *Positive Discipline in the Christian Home* stands as a refreshing change. The book offers both the novice and the experienced parent a clearly outlined, understandable, and sensible philosophy of parenting, complete with step-by-step implementation. Weaving Biblical wisdom with the proven theories of Alfred Adler and Rudolf Dreikurs, this book seamlessly blends the best tenets of faith-based living with the insights of modern psychologists, achieving a readable, down-to-earth, and invaluable guide for parents who want to raise great kids."

~ Diane Cooper, EdD, retired head of
Saint Edward's School, Vero Beach, Florida

"*Positive Discipline in the Christian Home* is the answer to every parent's prayer! It is packed with real life examples of the Biblical model of parenting and is a valuable tool for parents to use in their quest to raise children 'who live up to the full measure of Christ.'"

~Brenda Bird, pastor's wife, parenting educator,
motivational speaker

"Parents are God's personal representatives on earth to give each child a special blessing and stamp of approval. This book empowers you to do just that!"

~Tim Timmons, pastor of New Community Church,
author of *Roadmap to RICHE$*,
Los Angeles talk-show host

POSITIVE DISCIPLINE
In The Christian Home

USING THE BIBLE TO NURTURE RELATIONSHIPS, DEVELOP CHARACTER, AND STRENGTHEN FAMILY VALUES

Mary Hughes, MHR, and Mike Brock, LPC, with Jane Nelsen, EdD

EMPOWERING PEOPLE BOOKS

ISBN 978-0-9836052-3-2

Contents

To my family, who continue to be
living letters to me from Christ
(2 Corinthians 3:2-4).
—Mary

To my parents, Tom and Doris Brock,
who first introduced me to the teachings of Jesus.
—Mike

To my parents, Uriah Farrell (Woody) Wood and Agnes Laney Wood,
who taught me about unconditional love.
—Jane

A Special Acknowledgement

We wish to thank **Cheryl Erwin**, our colleague, friend, and coauthor on the original edition of *Positive Discipline in the Christian Home*. Cheryl contributed immensely both as lead author and synthesizer of our writings. She took our separate contributions and wove them into a coherent narrative, giving the book its signature style. *Positive Discipline in the Christian Home* could not have been written without her creative leadership and guidance. You can learn more about Cheryl's work at www.cherylerwin.com.

Acknowledgements

Acknowledgements are not easy because we are influenced and helped by too many to remember—and we don't like leaving anyone out. However we will start with Julie Pope, who over 25 years ago gave Jane Nelsen an outline of Biblical Scriptures she used while teaching Positive Discipline in her Presbyterian Church in Sacramento, California. Since then several people have told us how compatible Positive Discipline and Adlerian Principles are with the teachings of Jesus.[1] In part, it is this compatibility between Christian Principles and Positive Discipline that led to the creation of the book you are now holding.

We appreciate our families' graceful permission to share their life experiences—even their "mistakes"—which have become opportunities from which to learn. We also want to thank the thousands of parents who have told us that even though their children aren't perfect, they are so much better because of Positive Discipline—and that they and their children can now enjoy each other so much more.

A special thanks to Lynn Lott for helping us learn how important it is to teach experientially—and all the Positive Discipline Associates for continuing this vision through the creation of new activities and yearly training.[2]

Even though they lived before we had an opportunity to learn from them directly, we thank Alfred Adler and Rudolf Dreikurs for their teachings upon which Positive Discipline is based.

We would also like to acknowledge the pleasant experience we had as authors working together, and thank each other for the encouragement, support, and valuable ideas that were generated in this collaborative project to bring both Scripture and Positive Discipline together on the same page.

---

1. People of many different faiths have told us that Positive Discipline principles fit with their core beliefs.

2. www.positivediscipline.org

Introduction

A beautiful parenting story appears in Luke 2:41-52. In this familiar Scripture, Joseph and Mary have taken their twelve-year-old son Jesus to Jerusalem to celebrate Passover. After the feast, Joseph and Mary set out for home; they assume that Jesus is somewhere in the group of travelers, but after an entire day has passed, they suddenly realize that he is not there. We can only imagine their confusion and fear when they recognize that their son is nowhere to be found in all that empty land.

Joseph and Mary returned to Jerusalem; it took them three anxious, tearful days to find Jesus. When they did finally locate him, he was calmly sitting in the Temple talking with the elders. The Bible doesn't give us many details about that three-day search, but you can almost hear the distress in Mary's voice as she asks, "Son, why have you treated us like this? Your father and I have been anxiously searching for you." Jesus looks at her calmly and asks, "Why were you searching for me? You should have known where I was."

Now think for a moment. You are heading home from a family vacation when you realize that one of your children is missing. You turn the minivan around and rush back, but it takes you three days of frantic searching to find your missing child. When you do, he looks at you calmly and asks, "What are you so upset about?" Most parents would struggle mightily not to explode at such a moment.

You would assume that the Bible would give us a picture of appropriate discipline here. In fact, there are those who would say that this child has been willfully disobedient and should receive a good spanking—but no spanking happens. Instead, as far as we can tell, Joseph and Mary have a calm discussion with Jesus. And the story ends with Jesus returning to Nazareth with them, being respectful to them, and growing "in wisdom and stature, and in favor with God and men." (v.52) (Thanks to Fritz Mumm, a wonderful youth pastor and Positive Discipline teacher, for his interpretation of this Bible story.)

Most Christian parents want for their children exactly what Joseph and Mary seemed to want for theirs—that they learn respect and grow in wisdom, that they have the favor of God and men. But how does that happen? Secular and Christian bookstores overflow with parenting books, and concerned parents search for information. What *is* the best way to raise a respectful, responsible, capable child?

Listen for a moment as co-author Mary Hughes shares her "family-making" journey, as she and her husband searched for a style of parenting that suited them:

"When our children were born there wasn't much out there that squared with our Christian beliefs and made good common sense to me. As a child development 'expert' I was supposed to ooze confidence in parenting; after all, I'd gone to college to learn how to develop children, hadn't I? This became a family joke when our second pregnancy turned out to be twins; our oldest daughter was then just four years old. I had studied guidance techniques that should work in every situation, and most of the time these techniques worked pretty well—at least with other people's children. But I hadn't yet found any books or theories that focused on the heart of the matter.

"Nothing I ever studied in college taught me how to control my *own* three young children. Until I began to read Rudolf Dreikurs' *Children, the Challenge* and discovered Jane Nelsen's *Positive Discipline*, my parenting style wavered between that of a military general and the sweetest grandma you ever knew. Control, consequences, rewards for good behavior, inconsistency, and yelling when I'd reached my limit—I tried them all. I hadn't yet realized that what I wanted for my own children, as well as the children I taught, was an inner sense of security and a solid confidence that wasn't being developed through my strict but inconsistent style of parenting.

"Thankfully, my three children and husband survived the roller coaster years. *Positive Discipline* gave me the courage to be the kind of parent I had longed to be. In discovering these principles, I felt as though I had unlocked the treasure chest on the Candy Land game board. The challenges I faced could actually be met with consistent, calm, courageous steps—one step at a time. I grew into a more confident, creative, and loving parent. I would never be perfect, but this ministry God had prepared my husband and me to share, within our own home and in our church, was not based on perfection. It was based on the foundation of a loving God who, through His grace and mercy, showed us another way. And with what Dreikurs calls the "courage to be imperfect," my husband and I found our parenting hearts.

"Mistakes became opportunities to learn; our parenting style began to be both firm and kind without veering to the extremes (at least, not as often). Consequences became 'solutions' that often involved our children's input through family meetings or joint problem-solving sessions. Mutual respect was earned rather than expected or taken for granted. Responsibilities and rights became hallmarks of growth, rather than rewards doled out by adults. We saw Positive Discipline as applied Scripture.

"As we studied the Scriptures, we asked 'What Would Jesus Do?' long before the phrase was coined by the current age. In the '70s we participated in a Bible study where we read Charles Monroe Sheldon's book, *In His Steps,* originally published in 1896. This Bible study transformed our hearts, and ultimately our family, as we looked for help to a God who really cares. Gary and I still teach parenting classes at our church even though our children are grown and we have grandchildren, because we are still learning and growing in our knowledge of how God invites us to relate to each other here on earth."

As Mary discovered, parents are never perfect. Neither are their children. But it isn't necessary to be perfect to raise children who can love and walk with God, have healthy, happy relationships, and become capable, competent adults. The Bible is filled with messages of hope, inspiration, and everyday wisdom to guide families in their journey together. This book can give you some concrete, practical skills to use along the way.

This book is not intended to give you "the" answer. It *is* intended to help you fulfill God's purpose for the children He has entrusted to you; it is designed to encourage you to think about parenting as a long-term process rather than daily crisis intervention. And we, the authors, hope that the principles and tools of Positive Discipline will give "legs" to your spiritual beliefs—real skills that you can use to develop faith, respect, wisdom, and courage in the children you love so deeply.

Parenting, as you have undoubtedly discovered, is not an easy task. And most parents wonder from time to time whether they're doing the "right" thing. Christian parents in particular strive not only to guide their children's behavior, but to strengthen and affirm their children's faith and trust in God. As you will learn, mistakes are part of the learning process, for parents as well as for children—we all make them. Isn't it wonderful to know that God is quick to forgive, and to offer strength and encouragement to those who ask?

Parents have both a marvelous privilege and an awesome responsibility. We love our children so deeply, and yet the task of raising them well sometimes feels overwhelming. Positive Discipline can offer ideas and skills that will help, but you must supply the faith, the courage, and the steadfast love.

Abraham Lincoln wrote, "I remember my mother's prayers and they have followed me. They have clung to me all my life." Let us have faith that our prayers will cling to our children, and that we can love them enough to teach, guide, encourage, and enjoy them while they are in our care. Let us begin.

Chapter 1

What is Discipline?

The unifying characteristic of Christians across the globe is their love for Jesus Christ. Jesus was both kind and firm as he taught the principles of a loving gospel. It is this Christ-like quality that we hope parents will use as they raise their children to become loving members of their family, their community, and of God's kingdom.

Some people have asked, "Isn't it an oxymoron to say that discipline can be positive?" Not if you understand the true meaning of discipline. Discipline and punishment are not synonymous, as many people believe. The word "discipline" comes from the Latin *discipulus,* which means pupil or learner, and *disciplini*: "A follower of truth, principle, or a venerated leader; to teach." We want our children to be learners and followers of the truth and Christian principles, and to see Jesus Christ as their venerated leader.

Positive Discipline is a method of teaching and training through love. Jesus said, "A new command I give to you: Love one another. As I have loved you, so you must love one another. By this all men will know that you are my disciples, if you love one another." (John 13:34-35) Note that the command to love one another, in and of itself, was not new. The Old Testament law clearly taught "love your neighbor as yourself." (Leviticus 19:18, 34) What was *new?* He commanded His followers to love others "as I have loved you." Jesus was asking us—parents, teachers, and children alike—to model our love for each other and our lives after His. It is within this framework of Jesus' love—kind and firm love—that Positive Discipline operates. You will see throughout this book how Jesus and his disciples modeled true discipline (i.e., teaching, training, and discipleship).

> *Jesus was both kind and firm as he taught the principles of a loving gospel.*

Touching the hearts and spirits of our children is the objective of Positive Discipline. 2 Timothy 1:7 says, "For God did not give us a spirit of timidity, but of power, of love, and of self-discipline." Children need to develop self-discipline, not blind obedience that comes only from fear of punishment. Their behavior must be guided by godly principles. The New King James Version says, "For God did not give us a spirit of fear…" John, Jesus' disciple, wrote, "There is no fear in love. But perfect love drives out fear, because fear has to do with punishment." (1 John 4:18a)

A word about faith: it is not our purpose as authors to decide what you should believe about God, His church, or what constitutes the "right" lifestyle choices. These are decisions parents must make for themselves and for their own families. We do encourage you, however, to give serious thought to the message and values you want your children to cherish as they grow to adulthood. Those principles, like those we have already referred to, should become a part of every interaction you have with your children. A good church, a wise pastor, and a community of faith to support you will help you and your children live your faith each day of your lives together.

Practicing Discipline That Teaches

Discipline that teaches and trains through Christ's love must meet the following five criteria. Effective discipline:

1. Teaches children to love God and develops valuable scriptural, social and life skills. (Respect, concern for others, problem solving, and cooperation as well as the skills to contribute to the home, church, school or larger community.)
2. Helps children feel a sense of connection. (Belonging and significance)
3. Is mutually respectful and encouraging. (Kind and firm at the same time.)
4. Is effective long-term. (Considers what the child is thinking, feeling, learning, and deciding about himself and his world—and what to do in the future to survive or to thrive.)
5. Invites children to discover how capable they are. (Encourages the constructive use of personal power and autonomy.)

Teaching and Training

Bring your children up in the training and instruction of the Lord.

(Ephesians 6:4)

Train a child in the way he should go and when he is old he will not turn from it.

(Proverbs 22:6)

First and foremost, Christian parents want their lives and discipline methods to help their children learn to love God, to model for them a Christ-like life, and to teach them social, spiritual, and life skills. All Christians believe they should train a child in the way he should go, yet most wonder about how they can accomplish the fulfillment of this Scripture. What kind of parenting ensures that a child will become a responsible, capable adult who can choose to love and follow God all his life? Will strict parenting ensure the way he should go? What about loving your child so much that you grant every wish? Will that ensure such gratitude that he will not turn from the way he should go? How about lectures? Are your children listening intently to everything you say and absorbing it for the fantastic wisdom you have to offer?

We don't think so. We don't think any of these methods are helpful because they don't consider the "long-range" results. They don't consider what the child is deciding at each step along life's journey. Oh yes, punishment works if you care more about stopping the behavior right now than about what mistakes can teach the child (and you, as his parent) about how to be more respectful the next time. And rewards will often motivate compliance—at least for a while. But what is your child deciding for the future? Giving in to a child may provide a temporary reprieve from the temper tantrums, but again, what is the child deciding for the future? It is the decisions children make—about how to find love and belonging, about faith, about relationships (that form their personalities) from which they will not turn.

Children Are Always Making Decisions

It has been said that a child's personality is formed by the time he or she is five years old. Many people fail to understand this because they don't understand the power of early decisions. Even though they are not consciously aware of this fact, children are always making decisions about:

Who they are—good or bad, capable or incapable, worthwhile or worthless?

What others are like—friendly or threatening, supportive or non-supportive, loving or unloving?

What "works" in this family? How do I find belonging and significance?

And although they are not consciously aware of it, all children make decisions that go something like this:

I am _____.

Therefore I must _____ in order to survive or to thrive.

How might children fill in that blank? Some may decide, "I'm not capable, so I will give up and slide through life." Others may decide, "I'm not capable now, but I will do everything I can to someday prove that I am." Still others may decide, "I'm not capable of doing good, but I can sure be special by doing bad." Another may decide, "I'm not capable, but I can manipulate others into taking care of me." We could go on and on.

It's important to recognize that children are not consciously aware of the decisions they are making. They are simply attaching meaning to the experiences they have in life, building for themselves an "unwritten rule book." There are as many different decisions as there are children. The point is that too many parents do not consider the fact that their children are making decisions about behavior and what "works" that will affect their future beliefs and behavior.

What Would You Decide?

Hank said to his wife, Letty, in a commanding, harsh voice, "You go to your room and think about what you did!"

Susan said to her husband George, "You forgot to pick up your shoes again. No TV for you for a week."

How would you respond if your spouse treated you this way? Would you say, "Thanks, Honey, I needed that. When you humiliate me and punish me in this way I feel so motivated and empowered to do better." Or, would you say, "I don't *think* so. Who do you think you are talking to me that way?" Or perhaps you would simply withdraw, building walls to protect yourself against the pain and humiliation you felt.

Discipline that Teaches is Respectful to Children and Parents

Show proper respect to everyone.

(1 Peter 2:17a)

So in everything, do to others what you would have them do to you.

(Matthew 7:12a)

> Where did we ever get the crazy idea that in order to make children do better, first we have to make them feel worse?

Everyone knows the "golden rule," to do to others as you would have them do to you. Children are "others" just as much as anyone else, so why do we so often fail to realize that this Scripture is applicable to them? Why do we think punishment would be any more effective with them than it would with us? Where did we ever get the crazy idea that in order to make children *do* better, first we have to make them *feel* worse?

Think of a time in your childhood (or a recent time as an adult) when someone scolded you, put you down, humiliated you, or did anything to make you feel small and worthless. Relive that event as though it were happening right now. (You will find it very worthwhile to take a minute to do this.) What are you feeling? What are you deciding about yourself, about the other person, and about what you will do in the future?

You may be feeling scared, rebellious, bad, sad, amused, angry, indignant, or many other possibilities. Based on these feelings, you are deciding something that will affect your future behavior.

You may have to dig to realize what you are deciding, but you are making a decision. You may be deciding you are worthless, or that the person doing this to you is not worthy of respect. You may be deciding to stop taking risks for fear of failure, or to avoid getting caught next time. You may be deciding to get even with this person as soon as you can, or you may be deciding to be an approval junkie and to do anything you can to get this person to love you. Again, remember, that although these decisions usually remain unexpressed and are not made consciously, they are powerful motivators of our future behavior.

Considering what a child is deciding about himself, his world, and what to do in the future is just one reason why we do not believe that punishment is the best motivator to inspire a child not to turn from the way he should go. We (and reams of research that are buried in academic journals) do not see punishment as an effective long-term parenting tool. Punishment is an external motivator and teaches children to follow the right way only when an "enforcer" is around, not because he knows in his heart it is the right thing to do. When we talk about raising children, we need to recognize that fear and respect are not at all the same thing.

Discipline That Teaches Must Be Effective in the Long Term

Train a child in the way he should go and when he is old he will not turn from it.

(Proverbs 22:6)

What seems to work in the moment too often does not work long-term. That is why we often say, "Beware of what works." Even though you may stop a child's behavior, what is your child deciding about himself and about what to do in the future? What is he deciding about you? We have found that most children are deciding to adopt one of the 4 Rs of Punishment:

1. **R**ebellion: "I'll show them they can't make me."
2. **R**evenge: "I'll get even by hurting them back."
3. **R**esentment: "This is unfair …. I can't trust adults."
4. **R**etreat:
   a. Sneakiness: "I won't get caught next time."
   b. Low self-esteem: "I really am a bad person."

Parents can avoid this only when they understand that children are always making decisions—and that the long-term effects are more important than the short-term illusions of success.

Another important point about long-term effects is to realize what your children are learning about responsibility. Think about it. When parents use punishment (and rewards), it is the *parents* who are learning responsibility. When these methods are used, it is the parents' job to catch children being "bad" to mete out punishment, and catch them being "good" to mete out rewards, but what happens when the parent is not around?

Oh, the child's mind may be filled with guilt if he doesn't do what he "should" do. However, we think it is much more effective if the child's heart is filled with a desire to go the way he should go because he understands the value of "the way" to himself and to others. This child will be motivated by love and logic, rather than fear and guilt.

Spanking

Some parenting books advocate spanking as a fulfillment of the Scriptural warning "He who spares the rod hates his son."(Proverbs 13:24a) However, Scripture tells us that the rod was used to guide the sheep and to keep them on the correct path, not to strike or beat them. In Psalm 23:4 we read, "Even though I walk through the valley of the shadow of death, I will fear no evil, for you are with me; your rod and your staff, they comfort me." Proverbs 3:12 tells us ". . . the Lord disciplines those he loves, as a father the son he delights in." Few parents (and even fewer children) are truly delighted by a good spanking.

> Scripture tells us that the rod was used to guide the sheep and to keep them on the correct path, not to strike or beat them.

The Scriptures that teach us about the "rod" look much different when you understand that the rod was used for guidance and discipline actually means teaching. The emphasis of Proverbs is on verbal encouragement and teaching. The whole book is framed as a father's words to his son, teaching him those "facts of life" that have nothing to do with biology. Again and again he pleads, "Listen, my son." Mother has an equally important influence: "Listen, my son, to your father's instruction, and do not forsake your mother's teaching." (Proverbs 1:8) The parent-child conversation is a warm one, and Proverbs 17:6 bears out what the whole book implies: parents and children are not meant to be adversaries, but allies in life who are proud of each other.[3]

Cheryl, a music minister in her church, was instructed by a well-meaning pastor to use spanking with a wooden spoon on the buttocks to discipline her three-year-old son. After one spanking, she found him sitting on his bed, hitting himself in the head while saying, "I hate myself—I'm bad." This was not the kind of decision she wanted her small son to make about himself. She began searching for other ways to provide loving, firm discipline and eventually found that Positive Discipline was much more effective in helping her child learn respect, cooperation, and self-discipline, and that it was more compatible with her belief in a God of grace and compassion as well as law.

As we've seen above, Jesus commanded us to love one another "as I have loved you." (John 13:34) Parents sometimes make decisions that are not truly in their children's long-term best interests because they "love their children." They may, for example, pamper their children because they "love" them, or constantly criticize them because they "love" them and want them to "do better." Jesus' actions were full of grace and compassion, were non-punitive, and were always based on love that teaches and encourages.

---

3. Compton's Interactive Bible. New International Version 1. 1996 Softkey Multimedia, Inc., a subsidiary of Softkey International Inc. 1996 The Zondervan Corp.

Christians are familiar with Jesus' response to the woman caught in adultery (John 8:1-11). They may not recognize, however, that this is another example of His non-punitive, loving method of teaching. While Moses' law clearly stated she must be stoned for her actions, Jesus took an entirely different approach. He allowed those condemning her to recognize the sin in their own lives and walk away without hurting her. Jesus stated that He did not condemn her; and He instructed her to "Go now and leave your life of sin." (v. 11) An important principle of Positive Discipline is to "focus on solutions" that encourage children (and parents) to change their behavior.

When we advocate the elimination of punishment, many people ask, "Does that mean you believe you should let children do anything they want?" Absolutely not! While permissiveness may "feel" better at the moment (for both parent and child), it is ultimately an unloving approach to parenting. It does not help children develop self-discipline, responsibility, cooperation, and problem-solving skills from an inner locus of control—the ability to do what is right whether a parent is watching or not. And it does not obey the Scriptural command that parents must teach and train their children.

In Deuteronomy 6:4-9 we are commanded to be *continually* teaching our children to love God and follow his commandments: "talk about them when you sit at home and when you walk along the road, when you lie down and when you get up." (v. 7b) So, you may ask, if not punishment, and not permissiveness—then, what?

> *Kindness (which implies a strong and connected relationship between parent and child) is important because it demonstrates respect for the child. Firmness is important because it demonstrates respect for what needs to be done—for order and structure within the family.*

Discipline that Teaches is Kind and Firm at the Same Time

Jesus showed His followers what it meant to be kind and firm at the same time. With the woman caught in adultery, His kindness was obvious when He kept her from being stoned to death. But Jesus was also firm. He didn't tell her that what she had done was acceptable. Neither did he ignore the offense. He commanded her to "Go now and leave the sin of your life." Jesus did not punish and he was not permissive. He was kind and firm at the same time. That is why you will hear this theme repeated throughout this book.

Kindness (which implies a strong and connected relationship between parent and child) is important because it demonstrates respect for the child. Firmness is important because it demonstrates respect for what needs to be done—for order and structure within the family. The following excerpt from the book *Positive Time Out and 50 Other Ways to Avoid Power Struggles in Homes and Classrooms* (Nelsen, Prima, 1999) provides examples of what doesn't work (and what *does* work) to motivate children to "go the way they should go."

Eight-year-old Jake didn't do his homework. His father confiscated his bicycle and told him he was grounded (negative time-out) until he got it done. Dad thought this was a logical consequence for not doing homework. Jake was so angry that he sat in his room and thought about how he would refuse to do his homework or do just enough to get by to get even with his father. He certainly wouldn't do his best.

Sixteen-year-old Emma didn't do her homework. Her father asked Emma for an appointment to talk with her and asked, "Which would work best for you as a time to get your homework done, 6:30 or 7:00 this evening?" (Giving Emma a choice allows her some power, which usually invites cooperation instead of defensiveness. Waiting even a short time before a discussion allows both adults and children some time-out for calmness instead of the kind of attack and defensiveness that often happens when a discussion occurs out of anger.) Emma thought she knew what was coming and chose 6:30 to get it over with.

At 6:30, Emma was surprised when her father started by asking, "I wonder if you love yourself as much as I love you?"

Emma laughed and said, "What are you talking about, Dad?"

Dad said, "Well, I just wanted to let you know how much I love you. Because of that, I have your best interests at heart. I just wondered if you love yourself as much and if you think about your own best interests?"

Emma was very suspicious. "Is this your way of conning me into doing my homework?"

Dad replied, "Why would I try to con you into doing your homework if you don't think that would be good for you? We both know I can't *make* you do anything you don't want to do. However, I am willing to help you explore what is good for you, and I'm willing to help you create a plan that works for you to accomplish what is best for you."

Emma said, "Okay, Dad. I'll do my homework." Dad offered his unconditional love and acceptance first (just as the Lord does with us), then invited Emma to discuss the problem instead of using lectures and punishment (which she would resist, resent, and rebel against). Emma quickly figured out that doing her homework would be in her best interest. If her Dad had again fallen into the lecture trap and shared what *he* thought was in her best interest,

Emma might have figured out just as quickly that "Dad doesn't know best!"

Dad replied, "Honey, it doesn't work for me to have to remind you all the time. That seems to create a conflict between us. I don't want to spend our time that way. You wouldn't agree to do your homework if you didn't know that is in your best interest. How about taking it a step further? You might find it helpful to create a regular evening routine that includes the best time for you to do your homework—one that would work for you and that would take me out of the loop. You can show me what you come up with tomorrow night. I have faith in you to know what kind of plan would work best for you."

Emma agreed. The next night she showed her dad the following plan for school nights:

3:30–4:00	Chill out after a hard day at school
4:00–4:30	Phone time with friends
4:30–5:30	Homework
5:30–6:00	Chill (and maybe help out a little) before dinner
6:00–6:30	Dinner
6:30–7:00	Finish homework if not completed
7:00–8:00	Favorite TV programs, reading, or other relaxing activity

Dad said, "Looks like a good plan. Now this routine can be the boss instead of me. I think you will find this kind of organization very useful throughout your life."

Why Children Don't Cooperate

Many parents don't believe their children would be as cooperative as Emma was. If these parents have established a pattern of power struggles instead of guiding their children to use their own power in useful ways, then they are right—the children probably won't cooperate. What parents usually mean by *cooperate* is, "Do what I tell you to do." This definition does not invite cooperation; it invites rebellion.

When children don't want to cooperate, it could be that parents and teachers have not created a cooperative environment where children are truly involved in creating plans and guidelines and brainstorming for solutions. Many children have more practice in trying to protect their "sense of self" through resistance and rebellion against being controlled than in self-control and cooperation.

Emma was used to having her parents turn the responsibility for her actions over to her. They had spent many hours in regular family meetings brainstorming for solutions to problems. Emma had been involved in creating routines (bedtime, morning, mealtime) since she was two years old. Her parents established this process early on in life. (We will discuss routines, along with other Positive Discipline tools, in Chapter 8.)

Child Developmental, Age Appropriateness, and Temperament

Growth and change are a part of being human. Parents recognize this instinctively, and when their children are infants, most parents pore over the charts and tables in parenting books to be sure their children are developing "normally." The Bible, too, recognizes that each person's abilities and perceptions develop over time: "When I was a child, I talked like a child, I thought like a child, I reasoned like a child. When I became a man, I put childish ways behind me." (1 Corinthians 13:11)

Parenting books often lack sufficient information on child development, age appropriateness, and temperament. In Chapter 5, we will explore why it is important to understand your child's development, emotionally, physically, and cognitively, and how it should affect your parenting decisions.

Is This Book for You?

"And so we know and rely on the love God has for us. There is no fear in love. But perfect love drives out fear, because fear has to do with punishment. Whoever loves God must also love his brother"

(1 John 4:16-21)

If you respect God's authority, stand in awe of His majesty, and respect His leadership, then this book was written for you. This book is based on reverence and respect for God and His commandments. We trust that in this book you will find hundreds of ways to create a relationship with your children that withstands the turbulence and testing that so often characterize the parent-child relationship. Through this relationship, you will learn together as a family to have a relationship with God (and with each other) based on love, teaching, and encouragement that "trains a child in the way he should go."

POSITIVE DISCIPLINE IS:

1. An attitude based on a philosophy of mutual respect: respect for the Lord, respect for the child, respect for parents, and respect for others.

2. An attitude of love that requires both kindness and firmness at the same time. Kindness shows respect for the child, while firmness shows respect for the adult and the standard of appropriate social behavior. Jesus was the perfect example of kindness and firmness at the same time. This is such an important concept (and one that seems so difficult for most parents to accomplish) that we will spend more time on practicing kindness and firmness at the same time throughout this book—and will provide many examples of what it looks like in practical application.

3. An understanding of child development and what produces long-term positive results, rather than short-term, punitive methods that may stop misbehavior for the moment yet produce long-term negative results. (More about that later.)

4. A parenting toolbox with many discipline tools that teach valuable spiritual concepts and life skills (such as concern for others, self-discipline, and problem-solving skills).

5. A method that fosters love, satisfaction, and joy in Christian families who desire to follow Jesus' example and leadership.

Chapter 2

The Challenge of Christian Parenting

"God saw all that he had made, and it was very good."

(Genesis 1:31)

> Scott and Jane Roberson are a young Christian couple intent upon raising their two children on a solid Scriptural foundation. They also want to raise their children with good common-sense principles of parenting. They see no conflict between the two—a solid Scriptural foundation and good common sense parenting—but they often find themselves surrounded by conflicting messages. They search Scripture and find images ranging from "spare the rod, spoil the child" to the loving father gently embracing his prodigal son. They listen to the many secular voices giving parenting advice and are confronted with a wide range of opinion, from excessive strictness on the one hand to permissiveness on the other. How can they be the best parents that they can be? How can they fulfill the tremendous responsibility they feel as they gaze at their young children? How can they discern wisdom amid all the competing voices? And how can Scripture help?

Parents have always wondered about the "best" way to raise their children. Some things never seem to change: children misbehave and challenge their parents' opinions and edicts and parents try to set appropriate boundaries and balance love with wisdom and authority. Somehow, though, the question of how loving parents can raise moral, responsible, respectful young people has never been more urgent—and the Christian community is not exempt. Violence has invaded our schools; the media and mass culture popularize values and behavior Christian parents find appalling. Technology in the form of texting, social media, and the Internet sometimes has a seat at the family dinner table. Never has there been a greater need for discipline, yet the old "tried and true" approaches such as spanking worry many conscientious parents and are met with disapproval and skepticism by the mental health community and child protection agencies. Committed, loving parents find themselves wondering, "Is there anything that 'works' that we can do with confidence? Can we discipline our children with respect for ourselves, for them, and for the Word of God?"

Positive Discipline is not only consistent with Christian principles, as you will discover in the chapters ahead, it will lead you to family harmony and joy at the same time that it enables parents to create a respectful, loving home. We believe that the parents who base their relationship with their children upon both the wisdom of Scripture and the principles and practices of Positive Discipline will experience that joy in their lives and will raise happier, healthier children. From the very beginning, the writers of Scripture gave us a model for this positive view of our world: when God viewed His creation after each stage of its progress, "He saw that it was good." These words serve as a model for how we should look upon the children in our care, whether we are teachers or parents . . . or both. How often have parents forgotten the simple truth that the world *is* good when parents work *with* their children rather than working against them?

For many generations, parents believed that goodness was something they had to impose upon children (and, in some unfortunate cases, beat into children). A parent's role, most people believed, was to punish, chastise, and browbeat (or worse) the children in their care, all in the name of raising them according to a code of child rearing that they justified on both secular and scriptural basis. Many children have been "disciplined" with punishment and rewards, while other parents choose a diametrically opposite path, raising their children in a permissive environment in the hope that their children would always love them. Not surprisingly, this approach doesn't work either. These parents do not realize the wealth of wisdom in the Scriptures that can be applied to parenting.

> The Scriptures provide wisdom, encouragement, and guidance that is as valid today as it was thousands of years ago, yet parents must develop skills to apply those Scriptures in this difficult world we all live in.

This world of ours has changed rather dramatically since the *Leave it to Beaver* days in which children were cheerful and obedient, spouses always got along, and life was simpler. While the world was never as simple as we sometimes like to think, for better or worse, it has definitely changed. Ward and June Cleaver have moved away and in their place are families of many different sorts. There are single parents and stepfamilies, families of many different cultural, spiritual, and ethnic backgrounds, all searching for the best way to raise their children. Both mothers and fathers often work outside the home, while children spend time in day care and latchkey programs. Technology has created a generation of children who are far more sophisticated about adult behavior and privileges than their parents were at the same age.

While the spiritual truths and principles Christians have built their lives upon have not changed, our communities, our schools, and our children themselves have. Families who want to raise their children on the teachings of Scripture and good common-sense parenting are confronted by challenges quite different from those confronted by their parents—and undreamed of by their grandparents. The Scriptures provide wisdom, encouragement, and guidance that is as valid today as it was thousands of years ago, yet parents must develop skills to apply those Scriptures in this difficult world we all live in. Is it possible to follow Scripture, live in the modern-day world, and raise healthy, successful, responsible children? The answer is "absolutely!"

Observers and experts offer many explanations for today's unique challenges. The symptoms are everywhere (divorce, crime, drugs, the pervasiveness of sex in our culture), and most people can easily point to causes (too much television, the Internet, and confusion about the role of religion in society). Sometimes the symptoms and the causes get confused and parents don't know what came first: did the status of organized religion decline because of the sexual revolution, or did the sexual revolution result from the decline of organized religion? But parents everywhere agree that there is cause for concern.

Responsibility and Cooperation

Positive Discipline is built on the principles of mutual respect and dignity, cooperation and confidence, and responsibility. But in today's society children have fewer opportunities to learn these attitudes and abilities than they had a generation or two ago. Families no longer "need" children as important contributors to their economic survival. Generations ago, children were active contributors to the family economy on our farms, in the family business, and in the home; they were their father's apprentices or helped with the simple chores that were the necessary ingredients of everyday life. Today, we no longer raise our children to contribute to their families and communities; instead, we raise them as recipients of the many things we give them. In a previous age, being sent to one's room was considered punishment. Today, the child's room is a giant toy box containing everything from dolls and trucks to televisions and computers, all given in the name of love, but all attained through no effort of their own. If we are inclined to punish today (and as you will learn, punishment is not nearly as effective as true discipline), it might be more effective to send our children *out* of their rooms!

Children learn responsibility by being given responsibilities and contribution by being given opportunities to contribute. In our fast paced, busy, affluent world, we have neglected to raise our children with the simple chores and responsibilities that were taken for granted in previous generations. Children, as well as adults, need to learn throughout their lives to "serve wholeheartedly, as if you were serving the Lord, not men." (Ephesians 6:6-7) Chores and responsibilities do take time from parents; after all, children rarely do things exactly the way their parents do. It takes time for training and time for just "being with"; parents these days are busy folks and it often seems easier and more expedient to just "do it themselves."

In many homes, children have become the center of the universe. Because parents love their children so much, they become their children's chauffeurs, driving them from soccer practice to ballet practice to church youth group to piano class and on and on, making everyone's lives more stressful than they need to be. All too often, there is no space or time for effort or even input on a child's part. Parents provide a lifestyle, entertainment, and enough advice to make independent thought and good judgment unnecessary. But is this sort of love wise?

Jesus said, "Let the little children come to me." We believe this Scripture tells us how important it is to value children and help them experience the sense of belonging they so desperately need (more about this primary goal in Chapters 4 and 7). Children should be invited to make meaningful contributions to the family, contributions that also give them a feeling of belonging and significance, as well as real life skills.

Well-meaning parents sometimes create a "catch-22" for their children: they deny them the opportunity to experience belonging and significance in their lives through meaningful responsibilities and contributions, and then criticize them for not contributing, cooperating, or showing responsibility. Parents fail to show faith in their children, and then wonder why their children have little faith in parents or in the values they teach.

Children do not learn responsibility when parents and teachers are either excessively controlling or permissive. (Note that *all* permissiveness is excessive!) Children learn responsibility when they have opportunities to experience being responsible in an atmosphere of kindness, firmness, dignity, and respect. Our image of effectiveness in teaching responsibility is that of Jesus, sitting among the children, tenderly instructing them through love. That is the positive approach.

Seven Keys

Parents often wonder whether their children can handle responsibility and cooperation. "They wouldn't do *any*thing if I weren't constantly reminding them," parents moan. Consider for a moment the Biblical story of David, who at a young age was responsible for tending his family's flocks. Yes, times were different then, but undoubtedly young David worked alongside his family until he had learned the skills necessary to maintain both his own safety and that of the flock, which represented his family's wealth and livelihood. In the process of doing his work, he found the opportunity to learn to know his God, and to have confidence in both God and himself. The same can be true for your children.

Jane Nelsen and H. Stephen Glenn, in *Raising Self-Reliant Children in a Self-Indulgent*

World (Revised 2nd ed., Three Rivers Press, 2000), identify the "Significant Seven Perceptions and Skills" necessary for developing capable young people. Children develop these skills naturally when they are allowed to work side by side with their parents, receiving on-the-job training while making meaningful contributions to the family. These seven keys to developing capable young people are:

- **Perceptions of capabilities**: "I am capable of facing problems and challenges and gaining strength and wisdom through experience."
- **Perceptions of personal significance**: "My life has meaning and purpose—who I am and what I have to offer is of value in the scheme of things!"
- **Perceptions of personal influence over life**: "My actions and choices influence what happens in my life and I am accountable for how I live it."
- **Intrapersonal skills**: The tools to respond to feelings effectively: self-assessment, self-control, and self-discipline.
- **Interpersonal skills**: The tools to communicate, cooperate, negotiate, share, empathize, resolve conflicts and listen effectively when dealing with people.
- **Systemic skills**: The tools of responsibility, adaptability, and flexibility necessary to deal with the environment, family, social, legal, and other systems in which we live.
- **Judgment Skills**: The tools to set goals and/or make decisions, judgment, and choices based on moral and ethical principles, wisdom, and experience.

Imagine that you could look into the future and see the adult your child will become. If he or she posessed all these skills and attributes, we're willing to bet you would believe you had done a good job as a parent. These seven perceptions and skills can serve as checkpoints for how effectively you are raising your children. Do your children see themselves as capable young people with a sense of belonging and significance in their lives and the perception that the choices they make—about their faith, their behavior, and their attitudes—do matter? Have you provided opportunities for them to develop the life skills of self-discipline, effective communication, responsibility, and judgment?

> *Do your children see themselves as capable young people with a sense of belonging and significance in their lives and the perception that the choices they make—about their faith, their behavior, and their attitudes—do matter?*

The irony is that in past years children had real life opportunities to develop these perceptions and skills through chores, on-the-job training at home, in the shop, or on the farm. They learned responsibility by being held responsible—and by making mistakes. (Many great-grandfathers can tell tales about forgetting to milk the cow and what happened afterwards, both to the cow and to them!) As you will learn, mistakes are often a wonderful opportunity to learn. But although children had the opportunities to develop those perceptions and skills in earlier generations, they usually did not get to practice what they had learned until they became adults themselves. Instead they were told to "do what I say, not what I do" and to remember that they should be seen and not heard.

Today, many of our children are being raised in environments in which they have no experience with these perceptions and skills. Permissive parenting that gives few guidelines, authoritarian parenting that does not allow children to make decisions, declining social supports, and an irresponsible media have produced children who may be quite sophisticated about the ways of the world but who are very immature in their ability to lead successful, effective lives. Positive Discipline can help parents train children with the perceptions and skills they will need to become effective men and women of capability and virtue; the words of Scripture tell us what those virtues should be.

THE SIGNIFICANT SEVEN

1. Perceptions of personal capabilities

2. Perceptions of personal significance

3. Perceptions of personal influence over life

4. Intrapersonal skills

5. Interpersonal skills

6. Systemic skills

7. Judgment skills

Parenting Styles

There are three approaches to parenting, or "parenting styles." Most of us are familiar with the authoritarian style; this is the "do it because I said so" school of parenting. Controlling, strict, and sometimes overly harsh, this was the usual approach in our parents' and grandparents' day. Unfortunately, many loving parents interpret the Bible to mean that this is their only option if they want to raise respectful, Godly children. An authoritarian approach can invite resistance, rebellion, or deceptiveness, and doesn't teach the ability to exercise self-discipline and wisdom. (What will children do when the authority figure *isn't* around?)

The permissive style, either of the neglectful or indulgent variety, is widespread in America these days. Permissive parents find it stressful to set limits and difficult to follow through; it is usually easier and more pleasant (at least for the moment) to give in to children's demands and to show love by showering children with toys and other material things. Unfortunately, pampered children rarely learn compassion, respect for others' needs and feelings, or true self-esteem. Many parents lack confidence in their parenting approach and flip-flop between excessive control and permissiveness, being authoritarian until they don't like themselves and then permissive until they don't like their children. Each parenting style is briefly summarized in the chart below. Positive Discipline, which avoids both permissiveness and excessive strictness, allows parents to practice firmness with dignity and mutual respect, and to teach independence with clear and respectful limits, cooperation and responsibility.

Beware of What "Works"

We often hear people say that they believe in strictness because "it works," and we would agree that it does—in the short run. Punishment will definitely stop the behavior for the moment. For that matter, so does permissiveness: when we give in and let our children do whatever they want they seem so happy—in the short run. But what happens in the long run?

Many parents and teachers firmly believe that punishment "works." After all, if you spank a child, ground him, shame him or humiliate him in some way, he usually stops what he is doing. Each child, however, is constantly making decisions about ways to find belonging and significance, what things mean, and how they can survive or thrive in their families. And over the *long term*, punishment usually creates one of the "Four Rs of Punishment":

1. **Resentment**: "This is unfair. I can't trust adults."
2. **Revenge**: "They may be winning now, but I'll get even with them!"
3. **Rebellion**: "I'll do just the opposite to prove that they can't make me do it their way."
4. **Retreat**: "I won't get caught next time." (sneakiness) or "I am a bad person." (which leads to reduced self-esteem)

Children are rarely aware of the decisions they are making in response to being punished. These decisions are being made on the subconscious level, and future behavior is based on those deep-seated decisions. Parents must be aware of the long-range effects of their actions and not be fooled by the short-term results.

```
┌─────────────────────────────────────────────────────────────────────┐
│                    PARENTING STYLES SUMMARY:                          │
│                                                                       │
│  Excessive Control       Order without freedom                        │
│                          No choices                                   │
│                          "You do it because I said so"                │
│                          (rather than "because it's the right thing   │
│                          to do")                                      │
│                                                                       │
│  Permissiveness          Freedom without order                        │
│                          Unlimited choices                            │
│                          "You can do anything you want"               │
│                          (indulgent permissiveness)                   │
│                          "I don't care what you do." (neglectful      │
│                          permissiveness)                              │
│                                                                       │
│  Positive Discipline     Freedom with order                           │
│                          Authoritative                                │
│                          Democratic                                   │
│                          Limited choices                              │
│                          "You can choose within limits that show      │
│                          respect for all."                            │
└─────────────────────────────────────────────────────────────────────┘
```

When parents use excessive control and punishment, they often justify their actions by the belief that the child needed the humiliation of the punishment in order to learn. But who ever felt better about himself or herself after being criticized and punished? Try to remember the last time you were criticized or humiliated. Did that criticism and humiliation cause you to say, "Gee, thanks; I needed that. I feel so much better now, and so willing to cooperate and do what I'm told." We didn't think so.

Children do better when they feel better. Where did we get the crazy idea that to make children do better we have to make them feel worse? Think about it. As we have seen, the golden rule applies to children as well as to adults.

The Positive Discipline Approach

Many parents don't like excessive control or permissiveness, but they don't know an alternative. They worry that their children will make poor choices or choose to abandon their principles of faith, compassion, and morality, but they get tired of lecturing, nagging, and punishing. What are the options for concerned Christian parents? Many simply do what they experienced in their own upbringing (probably excessive control), then feel guilty for doing to their children what was previously done to them (after they had sworn never to do that). Some go to the opposite extreme (permissiveness). But neither the disrespect to children of excessive strictness nor the disrespect to parents of permissiveness works effectively in the long run, so parents find themselves right back where they started.

But there is a third way, and that third way is called Positive Discipline. Positive Discipline takes the word 'discipline' seriously, recognizing that its Latin root, *discipulus,* means a disciple, a follower of truth, principle, or a venerated leader. The disciples of Jesus followed Him not because He threatened them with punishment, but because He invited them with love and called them to be better than they were. He inspired them to faith because He had confidence in the men and women they could become. He gave them responsibility and accepted that they would make mistakes and wrong choices. (Remember Peter, denying Jesus three times? Judas' betrayal of his Lord?) In the life and teachings of Jesus, we have the picture, complete in every detail, of what Christian parenting can be.

Positive Discipline teaches that what matters is that our children learn the values, characteristics, and life skills necessary to be contributing members of society and to build their lives upon God's truth. Positive Discipline is neither excessively strict nor permissive. It teaches self-discipline, responsibility, cooperation, and problem-solving skills, and it does so with dignity and respect for all concerned.

The Scriptural Model

Scott and Jane, the young Christian couple we introduced at the beginning of this chapter, are enthusiastic about the Positive Discipline approach to raising their children but have wondered how it fits with the model for discipline that Jesus Himself taught us. In fact, it is for Scott and Jane, and so many other parents and teachers who have expressed a desire to synthesize their Positive Discipline parenting with their Christian beliefs, that we have written this book. How *does* the Positive Discipline approach square with the gospel message that Jesus left for us 2000 years ago?

We must look at the words of Scripture and the lessons of Jesus to see what we can draw from them to help us raise and teach our children to be effective and capable citizens who follow the words of Jesus in their own lives. We will explore all of the Scriptures that deal with discipline in the chapters ahead, and in the end, each parent must decide for him or herself how to approach this critical issue.

> The disciples of Jesus followed Him not because He threatened them with punishment, but because He invited them with love and called them to be better than they were.

Jesus has indeed given us a new commandment, that we love one another. He is not a laissez-faire Jesus who says, "Do whatever you want." When asked by the Pharisees what was the greatest of the commandments, Jesus replied that there were two greatest commandments: "The most important one. . .is this: 'Love the Lord your God with all your heart, and with all your soul, and with all your mind and with all your strength.' The second is this: 'You shall love your neighbor as yourself.'" (Mark 12:29-31) This is a powerful statement, and it transcends the strict/permissive debate. Love is not controlling; commandments are not permissive. We are commanded to love.

Who are these "neighbors" that we are supposed to love? Could anyone believe that we should love our neighbors next door more than we love our children? The next question is, "How do I show love—healthy love that guides and teaches—to my children?"

Many parenting mistakes are made in the name of love. Some parents say they punish their children because they love them. Others say they are permissive with their children because they love them. As mentioned above, we believe that many parents are punitive or permissive because they don't know what else to do to "train up a child in the way he should go."

When we search the Scriptures, we see a compassionate Jesus who fed the hungry, cured the blind, forgave sinners, and welcomed back prodigal sons. We see a Jesus who welcomed little children and encouraged them to come to Him. He was neither overbearing nor permissive. His only criticisms were aimed at hypocrites who spent their days judging others, and when he forgave sins, he reminded the sinner to sin no more. We believe that no greater model for parenting and teaching can be found than that of Jesus Himself. The tools and principles of Positive Discipline are an effective program for making that model work today.

What Do You Want For Your Children?

It has been said that if you don't know where you're going, you'll probably end up there. It is certain that in order to succeed at the challenge of Christian parenting, you need to have a destination in mind. Close your eyes for a moment: think about the children who live in your home. Imagine that 30 years have gone by, and your children are now adults. Who do you want them to be? What qualities, skills, and attitudes do you want them to have?

We have asked this question of parents all over the country, from many different backgrounds, and from many different faiths. Their answers are surprisingly similar. They want their children to be moral, happy, responsible, and confident; to have integrity, healthy relationships, and a sense of humor. They want their children to be compassionate, wise, and to be firm in their faith. So the question becomes, if this is your goal as a Christian parent, how do you produce these qualities in your children?

The answer is that each parenting choice, each decision, each act of discipline and moment of communication should be moving your children in the direction of the qualities on your list. Your list, incidentally, need not be the same as anyone else's—but you do need to know your goals and thoughtfully and intentionally pursue them throughout the time your children are in your care. The tools in this book are not intended to tell you what your vision for your children should be: they are intended to help you achieve it.

Life Lesson: "He saw that it was good."

In working with your children and trying to raise them according to scriptural principles, do you find yourself seeing the negative side of their behavior far more often than the positive? Do you find yourself looking for things to criticize out of the mistaken belief that good parents are those that vigilantly watch for transgressions and faults to correct? Or do you look for opportunities to appreciate and encourage your children's gifts, abilities, and successes?

Mike, one of the authors, spent many years as a school principal who frequently counseled parents about their children. (He is now a therapist!) He would often help parents guide their children back on track and move toward more effective behavior, but from time to time he would run into a parent with a problem that appeared to exist only in the parent's mind.

Marnie came to Mike some years back to talk about her seventh-grade son, Bill. Bill just wasn't applying himself, complained Marnie. He just wasn't taking school seriously. She was very disappointed with him and wanted to know what to do.

Mike listened intently but couldn't help wondering if the Bill that Mom was describing was the same one that Mike knew. That Bill was a polite, quiet boy, well-liked by his peers and teachers; as best Mike could recall without looking at his academic record, Bill was doing fine, around a 'B' average. So Mike said to Marnie, "Well, tell me about Bill. What's he like at home?"

"Oh, he's a great kid," Marnie replied. "Pleasant, easy to get along with, will do anything for you, gets along well with his brother and sister. Really, you couldn't ask for a better kid. In school, he's making a 'B' average, the teachers like him, he's got lots of friends. Seems to be doing fine all around." And then a tear started to form and she continued, "I don't know why I feel that I have to be on him all the time . . ."

Marnie doesn't have to be "on" Bill all the time. She just *thinks* she has to. She thinks being a good parent means looking for Bill's faults and correcting them. True, this is sometimes a part of parenting, but it's just as important to notice and celebrate what our children do well, to catch them being good.

God saw that His creation was good. The apostle Paul told us "whatever is true, whatever is noble, whatever is right, whatever is pure, whatever is lovely, whatever is admirable—if anything is excellent or praiseworthy—think about such things. Whatever you have learned or received or heard from me, or seen in me—put it into practice. And the God of peace will be with you." (Philippians 4:8-9) Perhaps focusing on those things that are good and excellent includes appreciating what is good in our children. With God's help, we can learn to see the good in our children (and ourselves), if we don't already. We can model the behaviors that flow from our personal values and, when necessary, correct our children when they stray. But if we remember that God saw that it was good, and focus on that good, more often than not we will see that good in our children. And we will thank God for them.

Chapter 3

Family Atmosphere–The Foundation

Do you dream of a family atmosphere filled with conflict, rebellion, fighting between siblings, and general disrespect? Or do you dream of a family atmosphere filled with love, cooperation, respect, and spiritual growth? We know this sounds like a silly question and that the answer is obvious. We ask the question because, although we all want a loving family atmosphere, we often engage in actions (although well-meaning) that produce the opposite of what we want.

As we, the authors, look back on our own parenting, we are a bit chagrined at the many times we experienced conflict and power struggles with our children. Oh, it wasn't the majority of our experiences (thanks to our Positive Discipline attitudes and skills), but enough to create some regret. We wonder, "What was that about? Was there a way to avoid the moments of struggle and unhappiness?" We love our kids and they love us—so why would we have power struggles? Now we know. It is our hope that sharing some of the insights we have gained will help you avoid some of the mistakes we have made. Let's explore the elements that create the family atmosphere:

Element 1.Make Sure the Message of Love GetsThrough

". . . But the greatest of these is love."

(1 Corinthians 13:13)

We know you love your children, and you know you love your children; but do your children know you love them? Oh, you may think the answer is obvious, but you may be surprised at how often the message you intend is not getting through.

One mother decided to ask her three-year-old, "Honey, do you know I really love you?" With all innocence, her daughter replied, "Yes, I know you love me if I be good."

A teenager replied to the same question, "Sure, I know you love me if I get good grades."

It is obvious that these children are hearing a message of conditional love. But what does the Bible teach us about love? Love, it says in 1 Corinthians 13, is "patient, love is kind. . . Love always protects, always trusts, always hopes, always perseveres. Love never fails." If we are indeed to love one another as God has loved us (John 13:34), then we must love our children—and make sure they *know* we love them—even when they misbehave, make mistakes, or fail to live up to our expectations. A parent's love, like God's, must be unconditional.

Even the best parents sometimes forget the "bottom line" of raising children—our love for our children—and instead focus on their fears. If you dissect your power struggles with your children you will most likely find some fear lurking there—fear for their safety and well-being, fear that you aren't being a good parent, fear over control issues, fear about letting them get away with something, fear that they will fall victim to the many risks and dangers in this world of ours.

Yes, there will always be control issues (after all, parents—not children—are meant to be the leaders of the home), but think how different they will feel when the message of love is established. Yes, you are the parent, and it is your job to guide and lead—and to make sure your children don't "get away" with some behaviors. Again, your guidance and leadership will be totally different when built on a solid foundation of love.

Parental love has sometimes been given a bad rap. Love is often seen as wishy-washy and permissive. And sometimes, it is. Parents sometimes make choices in the name of loving their children that are neither healthy nor effective in the long term.

However, it isn't true love that causes problems, but things that are done in the name of love. Mistakes made in the name of love are often disrespectful either of the parent, of the long-term benefit to the child, or of the needs of the situation. In other words, the needs of the situation may require that a child experience the consequences of his or her behavior. (More about consequences later.)

Parents make a critical mistake when they become permissive: they pamper the child, or refuse to allow the child to experience the consequences of poor choices, meaning that little learning for the future takes place. Sometimes parents go to the other extreme and make the consequences punitive and shaming instead of loving. In Positive Discipline terms, loving discipline means being both kind and firm at the same time.

Element 2. Practice Kindness and Firmness at the Same Time

Kindness and firmness at the same time is essential to creating a loving and positive family atmosphere. Kindness and firmness at the same time is a foundational principle throughout this book, one that Jesus modeled in His own teaching, and is the result of unconditional love in action. In fact, kindness and firmness at the same time is the balance that keeps our love for our children from whirling out of control, becoming something else (such as control or permissiveness) in the name of love. Kindness prevents us from being too strict and authoritarian, while firmness prevents us from being wimpy and permissive.

Kindness and firmness at the same time is *mutually* respectful. Don't you want your family atmosphere to be one of respect? We mention kindness and firmness here briefly, but you will read much more about it in the chapters that follow. Like many of the concepts we teach, learning to remain kind and firm at the same time often requires a paradigm shift (thinking "outside the box"). It means the way we perceive and think about an issue must change, not just the words we use in describing it.

Element 3. Change Your Vocabulary; Change Your Actions

Consider the words of James: "Likewise the tongue is a small part of the body, but it makes great boasts. Consider what a great forest is set on fire by a small spark." (James 3: 5) Vocabulary is powerful. One word can contain a whole philosophy that requires certain actions. Change a word and your philosophy and actions will also change. Let's take, for example, the important word "discipline." Doesn't that word convey a whole philosophy complete with necessary actions? Many people assume that those actions include punishment, but as we have learned, discipline and punishment are not synonymous. Because most people believe they are synonymous, we will repeat that *discipline means a follower of truth and principle*—or "to teach".

> Kindness prevents us from being too strict and authoritarian, while firmness prevents us from being wimpy and permissive.

Punishment actually inspires rebellion, not cooperation, and teaching is not effective in an environment of threat and fear. When you accept the logic of this, you will eliminate the word "punishment" from your vocabulary. And you can imagine how your family atmosphere will change when it is based on discipline that inspires cooperation (a follower of truth and principle) instead of being the atmosphere of fear and/or rebellion that is created by punishment.

The word "consequence" can imply punishment or learning. (Although some people believe punishment inspires learning, we don't believe children learn positive attitudes in an environment of threat.) In a positive family atmosphere, children will be willing to explore the consequences of their choices and learn from them—if parents change some of their words and attitudes around consequences. Parents often say, "He should *suffer* the consequences of his behavior." Is suffering really the best way to learn? What if the word "suffer" was replaced with "experience"? Let's try it: "I know my child will learn from experiencing the consequences of his choices." Ah, doesn't that convey a totally different picture?

A fearful parent will impose consequences (punishment) that make the child suffer. This can be difficult for parents if those consequences are painful or upsetting to the child, because some parents think the most loving thing to do is to protect children from pain and upset. However, allowing children to experience the consequences of his choices, even when painful, can be a great learning experience. A loving parent will allow his child to experience the consequences of his choices in an atmosphere of empathy and encouragement.

A loving parent might help the child *explore* the consequences of his choices through gentle curiosity questions (see Chapter 8) that invite the child to learn in a loving atmosphere. Both fearful and loving parents mean well. Both parents have the intention to help their children learn righteous living. However, one will be effective and the other will not. Loving discipline is much more effective long-term than punishment. Loving discipline focuses on solutions.

Element 4. Are You Looking for Blame or Are You Looking for Solutions?

As we love as Jesus loved us, we have opportunities to demonstrate God's grace. Jesus did not focus on the past, but continually encouraged change and growth in those around Him. When He saw "a tax collector by the name of Levi sitting at his tax booth," He said, "Follow me." (Luke 5:27) Although it was well known that tax collectors filled their pockets by skimming off the top of the collections they made, Jesus did not focus on Levi's past mistakes. He stretched out His hand to Levi, to help him step out of that lifestyle into a new one.

> A loving parent will allow his child to experience the consequences of his choices in an atmosphere of empathy and encouragement.

Similarly, as you follow His example, your family atmosphere will be much more loving if you focus on solutions instead of blame. Many parents spend a great deal of energy and time trying to figure out "who is responsible for this problem?" instead of focusing on "how can we *solve* this problem?" Punishment is a word that implies blame; it focuses on the past and on making sure that a child *pays* for his mistakes.

Discipline focuses on solutions and helping a child *learn* from his mistakes. Discipline looks to the future, towards the skills and attitudes that will *prevent* mistakes and misbehavior. Again, discipline is loving, not hurtful, and is most effective when parents share a loving relationship with each other, and are united in their philosophy and practice, what we sometimes call a "united front."

Element 5. Put Your Relationship First

The primary relationship each Christian has is with God. As the Lord tells us in John 15: 4-5, "Remain in me and I will remain in you. No branch can bear fruit by itself; it must remain in the vine. Neither can you bear fruit unless you remain in me. I am the vine; you are the branches. If a man remains in me and I in him, he will bear much fruit; apart from me you can do nothing." If you have a relationship of trust and faith with God, however, what comes next?

In most American homes, children are the center of the universe. Parents devote enormous amounts of time, energy, and money to making children happy and raising them well. So many parents are appalled to hear that their marriage relationship should take precedence over their children. Often single mothers feel guilty if they put themselves before their children. Yet putting your marriage and/or yourself before the children is one of the best ways to create a loving family atmosphere. Of course, the children should be such a close second that who or what is first is hardly noticeable, but that slight difference is powerful. Children feel safe when they know that parents honor their relationship first. In fact, Children learn a great deal about respect, love, trust, men, and women by watching the example their parents set by their attitude towards their God, their marriage—and each other. "A cord of three strands is not quickly broken." (Ecclesiastes 4:12)

When the children come first they sometimes learn to take advantage. They may use their personal power to get their own way, instead of learning to be contributing and co-operating members of the family. They often sharpen their manipulation skills to pit one parent against the other. In other words, they may be as miserable as their manipulated parents. Show us a successfully manipulative child and we will show you a very unhappy child. On the other hand, a child who is treated lovingly, with kindness and firmness at the same time, is a happy and contented child (at least most of the time: after all, only God is perfect!). This child is learning that the world (her family) does not revolve around her, but that she is an important *part* of a very loving world.

Element 6. Avoiding Sibling Fights and an Atmosphere of Competition

One thing that seems to have a negative effect on a loving family atmosphere is sibling bickering and fighting. Why does this happen, and what can parents do to change it? You can start by looking at yourself. Inadvertently, you may be creating a fighting atmosphere.

The less competition there is between parents, the less fighting there is among siblings. Parents set the tone (atmosphere) for their family. If they fight, the children will fight. If they focus on solutions, even when they disagree, their children will learn to do the same—with parental guidance. However, children learn what they live (by example) much more than from what they are told.

Even though you don't mean to create a family atmosphere of competition and fighting, it can happen unintentionally until you understand that opposites attract—and exactly what that means for parents.

When a couple marries, there is one crucial difference of opinion and style that doesn't show up until after the kids arrive. One partner is usually just a little too strict. (No, it isn't always the man.) The other is just a little too permissive. (No, it isn't always the woman.) However, the permissive partner soon develops the attitude, "Well, I have to be permissive to make up for my child's mean old strict parent." And the other partner is thinking, "Well, I have to be strict to make up for the wishy-washy, wimpy parent." They get further and further apart (and argue about who is right and who is wrong) when actually they are both wrong. To be kinder, they are both being ineffective. Children do not learn the attitudes and skills they need to become happy, contributing members of society when they are subjected to either extreme.

As you will hear over and over again, "mistakes are wonderful opportunities to learn." The apostle Paul taught, "Forgive, as the Lord forgave you" (Colossians 3:13). He was not only talking about our need to forgive others, but our need to forgive ourselves as well. But our task does not stop at forgiveness. You can learn to value your mistakes for the opportunities they present you to learn and grow in both your skills as a parent and your walk with God. This is not a time to beat up on yourself. You can feel excited that at least you *know* you made a mistake—and that you can fix it by going back to Positive Discipline methods.

What a gift to teach your children that they don't need to be burdened with the belief that mistakes mean they are stupid, bad, incapable, or inadequate. Mistakes are neither fatal flaws nor unforgivable sins. Children can learn, along with their parents, to turn to God for forgiveness, to forgive themselves, and to forgive others. They can learn to say, "Wow. I made a mistake. I wonder what I can learn from this?" This is the encouraging and empowering "Positive Discipline Way."

Element 7. Remember: Mistakes are Opportunities to Learn

Seeing a mistake as an opportunity for learning is essential to creating a family atmosphere where children thrive. Instead of fearing blame, shame, and pain, they will know that their parents will provide a supportive atmosphere (and skills) for them to learn from their mistakes. An understanding of your own mistakes and why you make them will help you forgive yourself. With more awareness of your own "buttons," you may be able to recognize them sooner, know when your children are pushing them, laugh at them (and they'll disappear), or simply learn from them.

Element 8. Maintain an Atmosphere of Self-Understanding: ("Button Button, Who's Got the Button?")

We all have buttons. Our kids know what they are and they know how to push them. And when our buttons get pushed, we are likely to revert to the part of our brains that researchers believe is responsible for the "fight or flight" mechanism. When the only options parents consider are fight or flight, children will also perceive matters in those terms. It doesn't matter who got there first: no one will be taking time to reason, listen, or look for solutions. No matter what you learn in Positive Discipline, you are still a human being—and you will sometimes "lose it" and so will your children. The wonder of Positive Discipline is that it can help you understand *why* you and your children lose it, and what to do about it.

How does this relate to sibling fighting? Have you ever noticed what a "hot button" it is for most adults when one child hits another? And have you noticed the ineffective ways they often handle it? They usually yell at the child, "How could you do such a thing? I can't believe you could be so mean. Do you want me to hit you and show you how it feels?" Can't the parent see that he or she is doing the very thing the child is being scolded for? When they stop to consider it, most parents realize how ludicrous it is to watch an adult hit a child while saying, "I'll teach you not to hit people!"

Usually, adult irrational behavior isn't quite so blatant (especially when you're the one doing it). You may have a "justice button." You try very hard to make everything fair. How will your kids push your button? All they need to say is, "That's not fair!" And you start jumping through hoops trying to convince them the slices of cake are equal, that their turn for birthday presents will come soon, or that you do *not* favor their baby brother.

One father handled the "fair" dilemma by announcing to his complaining kids, "I don't do fair." Another father let his kids know he did not have a fair button by telling them, "The only thing that is fair in life is that it is unfair to everyone."

It is important to note that these fathers made these statements with a twinkle in their eyes and a smile on their faces—with gentle humor, not with sarcasm. By their example, they were teaching the importance of humor, which can sustain both parent and child during many a tense moment of instruction. Sarcasm, on the other hand, teaches just one thing—how to be sarcastic—and there's no place for sarcasm in loving relationships. Positive Discipline will teach you how to avoid *re*acting to your buttons and to *act* thoughtfully more often. You will learn skills to resolve problems when they arise, as they always do. And you will learn how to avoid pushing your children's buttons. ("Fathers, provoke not your children to anger, lest they be discouraged." Colossians 3:21, King James Version) One of the many skills you will learn is the value of positive time out, for you and for your children, to allow time to access your rational brain again.

Of course, you will make mistakes—unless you suddenly become a saint. (Wouldn't it be nice if perfection was so easily attainable?) You'll learn that mistakes are wonderful opportunities to learn—for you and for your children. So, have fun with your buttons instead of getting hooked by them. Positive Discipline will show you how.

Element 9. Maintain a Sense of Humor

Who wants a dour, sour, way-too-serious family atmosphere? Some people act as though laughter is sacrilegious. One of our favorite pictures of Jesus depicts Him engaged in joyous laughter. Some people say they couldn't imagine Jesus laughing, and that they think of him as always serious. Yet we know that Jesus attended a wedding at which he turned water into wine (not, as some would think, vice versa). The phrase "joyful noise" (what else could laughter be

> *...we should also remember to appreciate on a daily basis the great gifts we have in our families, our communities, and our everyday blessings, and to be sure that the message of love and gratitude always gets through to those we love.*

called?) appears numerous times throughout the Bible. And we have as our example the beautiful Scripture that tells us that God gives us ". . . a crown of beauty instead of ashes, the oil of gladness instead of mourning, and a garment of praise instead of a spirit of despair." (Isaiah 61:3)

When we are fearful, we lose our sense of humor and take things too seriously. Parents must remember, even in the most trying of moments, that "a cheerful heart is good medicine, but a crushed spirit dries up the bones." (Proverbs 17:22) When parents and children can laugh together, they create a family atmosphere of warmth and joy.

Element 10. Cultivate an Attitude of Gratitude

During the final phases of work on the first edition of this book, terrorists hijacked four planes and crashed them into the World Trade Center in New York City, the Pentagon in Washington, D.C., and the countryside of Pennsylvania. How many of the thousands who died that day left their loved ones with complaints about chores not done, missing homework, or the everyday failure most of us share to appreciate the blessings we have, including the people we love? These people never had another chance to hug their children—but we do.

Ephesians 4:26 tells us "do not let the sun go down while you are still angry." Perhaps we should also remember to appreciate on a daily basis the great gifts we have in our families, our communities, and our everyday blessings, and to be sure that the message of love and gratitude always gets through to those we love. Scripture encourages us to "Be joyful always; pray continually; give thanks in all circumstances, for this is God's will for you in Christ Jesus." (1 Thessalonians 5:16-18) Creating a family atmosphere of gratitude and appreciation, moment to moment, may be one of the greatest gifts we ever give those we love.

Element 11. Develop Faith — in God, in Yourself, and in Your Children

Children develop faith in themselves when you demonstrate faith in them. A child cannot develop a healthy measure of self-faith when parents mistakenly rescue the child before the child even has a chance to solve a problem. Nor can children feel an inner sense of accomplishment when a parent unwittingly shows no interest in the way the child is handling his problems. If *you* don't believe he can handle disappointments, how will your child develop the necessary courage and faith to do what must be done? This is why it is essential to create a family atmosphere of faith—in God, in yourself, and in your children. .

Most Christian parents work hard to create an atmosphere of faith in God. We teach our children about God's goodness and grace. We teach our children to pray to God and to have faith that he will answer their prayers. The key is to encourage them—and ourselves—to apply these teachings when they feel upset or disappointed, instead of lecturing or rescuing.

The family meeting (discussed in Chapter 11) is a good time to pray together and bring answers from God to the problem-solving process. This helps children bring their experiences of faith to practical application in the world. What a great way to be *in* the world without being *of* the world. ("Trust in the Lord with all your heart and lean not on your own understanding. In all your ways acknowledge Him, and He will make your paths straight." (Proverbs 3:5-6) As difficult as it can be sometimes, have faith in yourself and in your parenting. Learn all you can and then use your own common sense and the wisdom you will receive in your daily prayers with God.

We have learned that Positive Discipline really works—when we use it. And, when we don't, we create a mess. We have also learned that faith is the necessary foundation for a parent's ministry in his or her Christian home. The good news is that no matter how often you "blow it," you can always return to God's sure forgiveness and the Positive Discipline concepts to clean up the messes you've made. The opportunity to create an even better family atmosphere is possible when you model what you first learned from God—that mistakes are truly wonderful opportunities to learn. With God's grace and a Positive Discipline education, you will continue creating a loving family atmosphere.

Chapter 4

The Scriptural Backbone
of Positive Discipline

Most parents who read parenting books are looking for specific answers to specific questions: How do we get our children to behave? How do we keep them from making terrible choices as they grow up—after all, the world is full of drugs, alcohol, and sex. How can we encourage them to hold on to their faith and to live their lives with integrity? How do we get a little help with chores and the work of everyday life as a family?

Raising children is about far more than getting them to do what we want them to. Positive Discipline is filled with specific answers—tools and techniques you can use to make life in your family easier and more enjoyable for everyone—but relationships always come before techniques. As Jane Nelsen frequently says, "Connection Before Correction." All early learning happens in the context of relationships—and relationships form the foundation for discipline, encouragement, and teaching skills. Positive Discipline is based on principles that will enable you to understand and connect with the wonderful, unique human beings your children are becoming. It is out of this relationship of love, mutual respect, and enjoyment that the techniques will come—and you will find that as these relationships improve, your need for "techniques" will decrease. John Ruskin said, "When love and skills come together, expect a miracle."

> *Adler's approach to understanding human behavior provides a set of basic concepts that are effective, respectful, and scripturally sound.*

Positive Discipline is based on the teachings of Alfred Adler and Rudolf Dreikurs, pioneers in the field of family relationships and behavior. Adler's approach to understanding human behavior provides a set of basic concepts that are effective, respectful, and scripturally sound and offer a wealth of knowledge to help us understand both our children and ourselves. However, Positive Discipline is so much more than just discipline theory and techniques. In this chapter we will take a brief look at the basic concepts of Adlerian psychology that are the heart of Positive Discipline. You are the only one who can decide what you want for your children and family. We trust that you will discover a solid foundation for effective Christian parenting, whatever your own personal values, beliefs, or denomination.

Why Understand Adler?

Positive Discipline is based on Adlerian concepts, and it is important to understand how these concepts are compatible with the Bible. The core principles of Positive Discipline—respect, love, trust, cooperation, responsibility, and teaching—mesh beautifully with Scripture, and with the teachings of Jesus. They are, indeed, built "on Rock." (Luke 6:48) The foolish parent builds a house upon the sand—whatever approach is popular at the moment. The wise parent builds a family on principles that withstand the test of the growing-up years, and that produce capable, competent, happy adults, what the Scriptures call "raising up a child the way he should go."

The concepts described in this chapter (along with many suggestions for practical application in chapters to follow) will help adults and their children understand more about human behavior, and thereby increase the likelihood that adult-child relationships will be satisfying and fulfilling. You will learn why children misbehave, as well as how to use Positive Discipline tools to help children learn the important life skills and attitudes they need to become happy, contributing members of their families and communities. You will also see how adults can retain their authority, as Jesus did when he taught the truth to His followers, without neglecting the caring and compassionate side of parenting. Positive Discipline is not just for adult-child relationships; it's a message that speaks to every type of person-to-person relationship: marriage, the workplace, friendship, the ministry and life of the church.

Equality and Mutual Respect

The foundation of Positive Discipline is mutual respect, a principle essential to Scripture. In 1 Peter 2:17 we read, "Show proper respect to *everyone*: love the brotherhood of believers, fear God, honor the king (emphasis added)." Most people today do not have trouble with the concepts of mutual respect and equality until it comes to children; then many "red flags" are raised. "How can children be equal when they don't have the same experience, knowledge, or responsibility?" people ask. It may help to remember that when it comes to children, "equal" means "equally precious in the sight of God," not "exactly the same." The equality we speak of here is not based on age, experience, or some physical quality.

In Luke 18:16, Jesus says, "Let the little children come to me, and do not hinder them, for the kingdom of God belongs to such as these." Jesus further adds, in verse 17, "I tell you the truth, anyone who will not receive the kingdom of God like a little child will never enter it." In these verses, Jesus tells us that although adults may dismiss a child as unimportant, He did not see children this way. Adults often lose their childlike sincerity and openness as they mature and begin to seek success and importance in the world. God gives us a child's heart as an example to follow and respect.

Although children do not—and should not—have the same privileges and responsibilities as adults, they *do* have just as much worth and value to God as do adults. Alfred Adler and Rudolf Dreikurs are the modern-day theorists behind Positive Discipline, but the Scriptures built the foundation long ago. Adler and Dreikurs advocated equality for all people, all races, men, women, and children, a familiar concept in Scriptures such as Galatians 3:28: "There is neither Jew nor Greek, slave nor free, male nor female, for you are all one in Christ Jesus." The equality that Adler proposes is not a matter of sameness, however. Rather, all people are equal in their human need for love, worth, and dignity. Each person is unique and is precious precisely *because* of his or her uniqueness; each person has equal worth, no matter his or her age. And each person, including children, has basic needs such as love, belonging, and connectedness.

Consider this simple activity we often do in our parenting classes. We ask everyone to look for a dollar in their wallet. We give everyone a few moments to find the money and then ask, "How many of you went directly to the bill section of your wallet?" Most of the class locates a one-dollar bill. Occasionally there is a parent who only has ten dimes, or four quarters, or some other combination of coins; a few even say, "I don't have a dollar." We then point out how many different ways there are to make a dollar, each one worth exactly the same amount.

Then we ask, "In what ways are children equal to their parents? (Parents come up with answers such as worth, need for love, and the need to be nourished and nurtured.) "In what ways are adults different from children?" (Again, common answers are size, responsibility, experience, knowledge, and so on.) The concept of equality, drawn from both Adler and the Bible, is foundational to establishing family relationships that are built on mutual respect.

> *...when it comes to children, "equal" means "equally precious in the sight of God," not "exactly the same."*

Parents *expect* their children to respect them, but they sometimes struggle with the notion that they should first respect their children. Since "the fear of the Lord is the beginning of wisdom," (Psalm 111:10) parents sometimes think, "I'll just settle for having my children fear me." But as we have already seen, fear and respect are not the same. And in fact, fear can keep a child from learning self-discipline and integrity.

In past generations, children were considered inferior to the adults who raised them. For decades in our democratic society, during the industrial revolution days to present times, children have either been excused from all responsibility or given responsibility way beyond their years. They either had all rights or none, because adults have not fully understood the nature of democracy—or did not believe it applied to children.

There is a simple Adlerian equation that reflects the spirit of democracy (and democratic parenting): "R = C+C," which means "responsibility equals choice *plus* consequence." Parents sometimes err (with the best of intentions) by being either permissive or excessively strict when teaching responsibility. They either fail to hold children (or themselves) accountable for choices, or heap on humiliation and punishment (often disguised as consequences) when a wrong choice is made. When democracy works, we make choices and we experience the consequences of those choices, either positive or negative consequences based on the nature of the choice, while focusing on solutions.

Do You Win Over Children or Win Children Over?

Sometimes, in the name of equality and respect, adults have misused the concept of equality to *win over children* rather than to *win children over*. Winning over children makes children "losers." When adults use punishment or humiliation to coerce children to stop misbehaving, it may feel as though they have won. However, in the long term, the punishing parent loses because, as we have seen, children may become rebellious or sneaky, and usually fail to truly learn self-discipline, responsibility, cooperation, problem-solving skills, and all the other life skills they need.

It is no more effective to let *children* "win" by catering to their whims and moods. Being in either of these one-down positions generally causes children to become manipulative, rebellious, or blindly submissive. When parents opt for what 'works' in the short-term rather than choosing to raise children in ways that produce effective long-range results for their entire family, they will not be truly effective in helping their children become capable, confident adults.

If parenting were just a short sprint, there would be no need for the words in Scripture that, though they describe life as a Christian, could well be read with Christian parenting in mind: "… let us run with perseverance the race that is marked out for us. Let us fix our eyes on Jesus …who, for the joy set before him, endured the cross … Consider him who endured such opposition … so that you will not grow weary and lose heart." (Hebrews 12:1-3) *Winning children over* means gaining their cooperation while you are teaching responsibility, self-discipline, problem-solving skills, and social interest. Adults *win children over* when they have faith in their abilities and take time for training in essential life skills. Picture two figures on a see-saw trying to balance, and you have a visual metaphor of the Adlerian concept of mutual respect.

The Primary Human Need: Belonging and Significance

As Jesus was teaching one day, parents (who, after all, always want the best for their children) kept bringing their children forward for Jesus to touch. The disciples, trying to protect their teacher, rebuked these parents and tried to shoo away the children. Jesus left no doubt about how He felt: He was "indignant." "Let the little children come to me," He said, and "took the children in His arms, put His hands on them, and blessed them." (Mark 10:13-16) Jesus apparently did not believe that children should be "seen and not heard." Jesus knew children need a sense of belonging and significance as much as their parents do, and He was never too busy to help them experience it.

Adler and Dreikurs believed that the goal of all human behavior is to achieve *belonging and significance*. Misbehavior, as we will learn in Chapter 7, is based on a mistaken belief about how to achieve belonging and significance. The Bible gives us a clear picture of the relationship God desires with us. He wants us to follow His precepts because *we* have chosen His ways; in other words, He is willing to treat us with the same respect that He would like to receive from us.

God's desire for us is to experience family relationships that are as nurturing as they are affirming, as forming as they are freeing. The relationship Jesus built with his disciples makes it clear that we are created to be in relationship to each other. We were made to connect with the Lord, as well as each other, and Jesus has shown us the way by living a life that is a model for us today.

When parents understand that behavior is dependent on a child's sense of belonging and significance (which will be explained more fully in Chapter 7), they can help misbehaving children obtain their goals in more positive ways. You will feel differently about misbehavior when you remember that behind the misbehavior is a child who just wants to belong and is confused about how to accomplish this goal.

Encouragement

How often have you heard someone say, "What that kid needs is a little old-fashioned discipline!" For most folks, "old-fashioned discipline" actually means punishment. But believe it or not, a misbehaving child is actually a discouraged child. Because misbehavior grows out of discouragement, punishment will only add to the discouragement—and usually leads to more misbehavior. Only a child who *feels* and *thinks* better will *do* better.

Any tool, including the Positive Discipline tools, is worthless without an underpinning of encouragement, understanding, connection, and respect. Remember, our model as parents is Jesus Himself. In 1 Corinthians 13, we learn that the "most excellent way" of relating to one another is love—not a manipulating kind of love, but rather a love that is kind and gentle without losing its firmness and follow-through. Love is more than just a feeling: it must be a part of each parenting choice, each action, and the very atmosphere of our homes. Indeed, "without love we (parents) are just clanging cymbals or resounding gongs…" (1 Corinthians 13:1) As a child once said, "a parent is Jesus with skin on!" Encouragement—love in action—is such an important concept that we have devoted a whole chapter to helping you understand and apply it (More on encouragement in Chapter 9).

There Are Always Beliefs Behind Behavior

Human behavior always has a purpose, even when we do not consciously understand what the goal is. Our goals and beliefs come to life in our relationships with those around us. For children, that usually means in the family and in the classroom.

It's important to realize that the primary human need—belonging and significance—is not something children (or the rest of us, for that matter) can put into words or are *consciously* aware of. Sometimes children have mistaken ideas of how to achieve what they want, and behave in ways that achieve just the opposite of their goal. Think for a moment of an average male middle-school student. It's an awkward age: some youngsters have sprouted up, some have deep voices, while others continue to look like refugees from elementary school. Our 13-year-old hero wants very much to be liked by his peers—to be popular—but isn't quite sure how to achieve this goal. So he tries to act "cool," boasts about skills and possessions he doesn't really have, and generally behaves more like Ichabod Crane from "Sleepy Hollow" than the Prince Charming he imagines himself to be.

This often creates a vicious cycle: The more a child's behavior invites dislike and is reinforced through negative attention (lectures from the teacher, ostracism by peers, or nagging from parents), the more obnoxious that child may act. He wants to be liked, is confused about how to achieve that goal, and is beginning to feel discouraged—not a recipe for excellent behavior. Dreikurs explained this when he said, "Children are good perceivers, but poor interpreters." Our middle-school friend may even feel a sort of belonging: after all, he's certainly receiving a lot of attention. Strange as it may seem, for many children negative attention is vastly preferable to no attention at all.

In Chapter 7, we will talk more about how children choose these mistaken goals (which parents usually call "misbehavior") in their attempt to seek belonging and significance. We can learn to respond to a child's *beliefs* rather than just the behavior or the misbehavior. And that is when behavior truly begins to change.

Social Interest

There is a beautiful German word coined by Alfred Adler, *Gemeinschaftsgefühl.* There is no accurate English translation, but Adler finally chose "social interest." "Community feeling" is another possible interpretation. Social interest means having concern for one's fellow men and women and a sincere desire to make a contribution to society. It is the embodiment of a life of Christian love and service to the family, the community, and the world.

The American people united in a powerful expression of social interest in the aftermath of the terrorist hijackings in New York City and Washington, D.C., contributing resources and millions of dollars to the rescue effort and the families of those injured and killed. People stood in line for hours to donate blood, and drove across the country in hopes that they could find a way to help. Children sold lemonade and red-white-and-blue ribbons, and donated their earnings to the American Red Cross. That is social interest in action, and it is a quality our world desperately needs. Not surprisingly, it begins at home.

It is extremely important to teach social interest to children. What good is academic learning (or even excellent behavior at home) if young people do not learn to become contributing members of society? Families are the best places for children to learn the message of Philippians 2:3-5: "Let nothing be done through selfish ambition or vain conceit, but in humility consider others better than yourselves. Each of you should look not only to your own interests, but also to the interests of others." Let each esteem others better than himself. Look not after your own concerns, but let every man also look after the concerns of others. Your attitude should be the same as that of Christ Jesus." In other words, children, too, can learn to respect the needs of both themselves and others.

Rudolf Dreikurs often said, "Don't do anything for a child that a child can do for herself."

When parents constantly serve a child, they rob that child of opportunities to develop the belief that she is capable, the true meaning of "self-esteem." The first step in teaching social interest is to teach self-reliance. When children have confidence and skills, they are ready to help others and feel capable and confident when they do enter into this more interdependent relationship. As we will learn, truly loving your child may mean teaching him skills and attitudes, and then letting go with love while he practices those skills. We live in an age of super-moms and super-teachers, where children sometimes expect the world to serve them, rather than to be of service to the world.

It's time for a little personal inventory:

- How many things are you doing *for* children that could be done *by* children?
- How much of your family's time and energy is spent on things and how much is devoted to community?
- What are your children learning about generosity, compassion, and gratefulness?

Jesus modeled the servant's heart when he washed the disciples' feet. He bent down to do a menial job to demonstrate that *"*I have set you an example that you should do as I have done for you. I tell you the truth, no servant is greater than his master, nor is a messenger greater than the one who sent him. Now that you know these things, you will be blessed if you do them." (John 13:15-17*)* If parents do all the serving, they rob their children of opportunities to develop the seven skills and perceptions of capable adults we learned about in Chapter 2.

One way of encouraging social interest is by getting children involved in brainstorming (and doing!) the jobs that need to be done in the family. Parents can participate in the brainstorming, but it is amazing how much children can contribute when they are invited to do so. The more a child can contribute to those he loves, the more he can see that he *matters*. Mattering to someone is what living is all about. We will learn more about developing social interest through contribution in Chapter 11 on family meetings.

Mistakes are Wonderful Opportunities to Learn

Mistakes are often viewed as "sins" or flaws when they are actually just a part of the learning process. Parents are often at their best when they learn to use mistakes and life lessons as opportunities for teaching. Rather than doling out punishments, parents have the honor and privilege of bringing children before the throne of grace. As a parent, you can help children discover their need for a forgiving God by showing them the way, offering both forgiveness and opportunities to learn, correcting mistakes and misbehavior in the process.

> *Parents are often at their best when they learn to use mistakes and life lessons as opportunities for teaching.*

Close your eyes and remember the messages you received from parents and teachers about mistakes when you were a child. What were those messages? To make this exercise more powerful, you may want to write them down. When you made a mistake, did you receive the message that you were stupid, inadequate, bad, a disappointment, or a klutz? Close your eyes again, and let yourself remember a specific time when you were criticized for a simple mistake. What were you deciding about yourself and about what to do in the future?

Remember, you were not aware that you were making a decision at the time, but when you look back it is usually obvious what decisions you were making. Some people decide they are bad or inadequate. Others decide they should not take risks for fear of humiliation if their efforts fall short of perfection. Too many decide to become "approval junkies" and try to please others, at great cost to their self-esteem. And some decide they will be sneaky about their mistakes and do everything they can to avoid getting caught.

Are these messages and decisions that will produce healthy, happy people? Of course not.

When parents and teachers give children negative messages about mistakes, they usually mean well. They are trying to motivate children to do better. Perhaps they haven't taken time to think about the long-range results of their methods. So much parenting and teaching is based on worldly fear. Parents may fear they aren't doing a good job if they don't *make* children do better. Too many are more concerned and afraid about what the neighbors or the folks at church will think than about what their children are learning. Others are afraid that children will never learn to do better if they don't instill fear and humiliation in them. Most are afraid because they don't know what else to do, and fear that if they don't inflict blame, shame, and pain, they will be acting permissively. Often parents cover up their fear and confusion by becoming more controlling.

> *Model the courage to accept imperfection as a step along the path to growth and remember that your own attitude and actions are your children's best teachers.*

As we have already discovered, there is another way. Many of the stories in this book are about the mistakes we have made with our own children. They have survived, and so have we—and often those mistakes became opportunities for closeness, understanding, and growth.

Many of our children's mistakes happen because we haven't taken time for training and encouragement. We often provoke rebellion instead of inspiring improvement. Model the courage to accept imperfection as a step along the path to growth and remember that your own attitude and actions are your children's best teachers.

Teach your children to be willing to "Come Unto Jesus," as the Christian songwriter Dallas Holm says:

> *"Come unto Jesus; give Him your life today.*
> *Oh, I know there are things in your life you think He can't forgive,*
> *but He'll forgive and forget, my friend, and show you how to live."*
> (The Benson Company, © by Dimension Music,
> words and music by Dallas Holm.)

Bring your mistakes to the Lord, and your child will see the sense in doing the same. Avoid hanging on to guilt; lay it down and leave it there. Hanging on to the past creates a weight that keeps you from living in the present and from being able to meet the future.

Make Sure the Message of Love Gets Through

The goal of discipline is "to teach" and to teach in such a way that your child respects both himself and you. Discipline may be hard in the lesson it teaches, but should never be so hard as to take the love out of the teaching. The Adlerian concepts described in this chapter and the Positive Discipline tools you will find throughout this book provide the foundation for understanding behavior and developing the attitudes and methods necessary to help children develop the life skills they will need when they venture out into the world.

Think for a moment: Isn't it better to use the mistakes children make as learning tools while they live in your home and attend your church, than to have them make mistakes with a larger price tag after they are no longer in the shelter of your love? The day will come—sooner than any of us ever expect—when our children will make their way into the world. You will want them to have their full armor on, prepared to meet the challenges they will experience in adult life.

Ephesians 6:10-17 encourages Christians to be strong in the Lord and in his mighty power, to put on the full armor of God. As a Christian, you should stand firm with the belt of truth buckled around your waist, with the breastplate of righteousness in place, and with your feet fitted with the readiness that comes from the gospel of peace. We are to take up the shield of faith, the helmet of salvation, and "the sword of the Spirit, which is the word of God."

CORE PRINCIPLES OF POSITIVE DISCIPLINE

- Mutual respect and equality

- Belonging and significance

- Win children over instead of winning over children

- Encouragement

- There are always beliefs behind behavior

- Social interest

- Mistakes are opportunities to learn

- Certainty that the message of love gets through

Built On Rock

"I will show you what he is like who comes to me and hears my words, and puts them into practice. He is like a man building a house, who dug down deep and laid the foundation on rock. When a flood came, the torrent struck the house but could not shake it, because it was well built."

(Luke 6:47-48)

Perhaps these words are the heart's prayer of all Christian parents; that their children grow up to become people of compassion and confidence, who build their lives and the lives of their own children on a firm foundation. The Bible and Positive Discipline can help you put your vision for your children into everyday, effective action. The chapters ahead will show you how.

Chapter 5

"But the Lord Looks at the Heart": Getting Into Your Child's World

Not only do Christian parents love their children, they also know that "children are a heritage from the Lord, and the fruit of the womb is his reward." (Psalm 127:3, KJV) Happy, we are told, is the man who has a "quiver full of them." Yet sometimes life in a busy family is anything but peaceful and joyous. Both children and parents have too much to do, feel stressed and anxious, and sometimes feel that no one truly understands them. If a sense of belonging and significance—of connection to the people you love—is essential to being happy and healthy (and we believe that it is), then perhaps the most important parenting tool is one parents sometimes overlook.

Children are more than their behavior. Their personalities are formed by more than just "nature" (the qualities and characteristics they have inherited from you) and "nurture" (the environment they grow up in). Each child has a God-given spirit—a soul. Although they may resemble the parents who gave them birth ("You're *just* like your father," we say with a mixture of fondness and exasperation), children inexorably become something unique: they become *themselves*.

And the process begins much sooner than you might think.

1 Samuel 16:7 tells us that "the Lord does not look at the things man looks at. Man looks at the outward appearance, but the Lord looks at the heart." Wise parents learn that they, like God the Father, must see into each child's heart. Getting into your child's world— understanding his development, his thoughts and dreams, his strengths and his weaknesses—will strengthen your relationship with him, and may even make a great deal of "discipline" unnecessary.

> *...children inexorably become something unique: they become themselves.*

Most parents worry about the choices their children will make as they grow and become more independent, about the risks and challenges they will inevitably face. Most parents recognize that eventually their children will move far beyond their immediate control and will rely on their own judgment as they journey through life. We know that children are always making decisions, and that the decisions they make about themselves, their parents, and life itself are crucial in shaping the people they become. How can loving parents understand what those decisions are? How do you get to know—*really* know—the people your children are becoming? What tools can a wise parent use to look upon a child's heart?

Understanding Development and Developmental Appropriateness

The Bible recognizes that each person's abilities and perceptions develop over time: "When I was a child, I talked like a child, I thought like a child, I reasoned like a child. When I became a man, I put childish ways behind me." (I Corinthians 13: 11) Sometimes parents have highly unrealistic expectations of what their children should be able to do at each stage of their lives. After all, few parents have the opportunity to study child development before they have that first baby. Yet knowing how children grow, how their brains and bodies develop, and what they are truly able to understand and do can help parents know the difference between outright misbehavior and behavior that, while annoying or frustrating, is appropriate for that child's age.

Understanding development also helps parents understand that a child's misbehavior is rarely as "personal" as it feels; parents can "unhook" emotionally and respond in thoughtful, kind, firm ways to the challenges of a child's behavior. They can also comprehend more fully why it is always more effective to use discipline to *teach* than to punish.

Ages and Stages

A truly comprehensive look at the ways children develop physically, emotionally, and cognitively is beyond the scope of this book, but let's take a flying tour through the years and explore some of the traits and challenges common to children of different ages.

Birth to Three Years

Did you know that when an infant is born, the only part of her brain that is complete is the brain stem (the part that controls involuntary functions like heart rate and respiration)? The rest of a child's brain continues to grow—to physically expand—within her skull for the first three years of her life. This is why those first years of life are so critically important in forming your child's sense of right and wrong, her self-esteem, and her sense of belonging and significance. Neurobiologists now tell us that *all* important early learning happens in the context of *relationships*—and it's absolutely true.

Erik Erikson, a true pioneer in understanding the way children grow, believed that the primary challenge in the first year of life is establishing a sense of trust. Children bond with their parents (or fail to); they learn that when they cry, when they are hungry or wet, or when they need comfort, someone comes to help them. This trust is the foundation for a lifetime of love and respect between parent and child. While you might be able to spoil a child if you never put her down or pick her up every time she hiccups, discipline is rarely necessary during the first six months of life.

At this stage it is important for parents to understand the difference between needs and wants. What an infant needs is contact and warmth, laughter and the sound of a parent's voice, a confident response to her needs, and comfort when she is upset. However, that last need (comfort) is the tricky one. There is a fine line between giving comfort that encourages and comfort that discourages. For example, an infant may sound upset while soothing herself to sleep. (Yes, crying can be a self-soothing mechanism.) But falling asleep by herself (a natural bodily function) encourages her to develop confidence in herself. Parents who think they need to help their children fall asleep are actually discouraging their children because children may not develop confidence in themselves. Instead they develop the belief that, "I can't fall asleep by myself." This will develop into a habit that will cause many problems—upset children and harried parents—in a very few months.

These first few months often require more *self*-discipline on the parents' part. As your child grows, discipline (which means, you may recall, simply "teaching") will become an important part of her life—especially as she moves into her second year.

Erikson called this year the year of *autonomy*. Children begin to figure out that they are separate people from their frazzled moms and dads, which is what makes the word "no" so wonderfully attractive! Believe it or not, two-year-olds are not "terrible"; they are simply exploring the world around them, learning to feel comfortable in their own small bodies, and developing a knowledge of language, social skills, and the "family rules"—tasks that are far more complicated than

> *...trust is the foundation for a lifetime of love and respect between parent and child.*

you might think. Two-year-olds need patience, repetition, and action (this may mean quietly leading them to what they need to do, such as stay out of the street) instead of words. In fact, what they need at two is what they will need throughout their lives: kind, firm discipline that teaches.

Three is the year of *initiative*. At three, children begin to connect cause and effect (in fact, before this age such parenting tools as time out and consequences rarely make sense to a child in the way adults assume they do) and can begin to make plans—and carry them out. Adults become frustrating folks who just get in the way of what "me wants." Parents of three-year-olds know all too well what it feels like to have a debate with someone who only comes up to your kneecap—and to lose! Again, kindness and firmness are the foundation for effective discipline. (For more information on development and parenting of children in their early years, see *Positive Discipline: The First Three Years,* Nelsen, Erwin, and Duffy, Three Rivers Press, 2008.)

The Preschool Years

As children grow towards school age, their world widens. They develop better language skills and their unique personalities begin to shine. They can form friendships, and they begin to explore the world outside their family. They are likely to go to preschool, and can begin to cooperate with parents in family meetings and problem solving. They are not, however, "little adults," and are still not able to think and reason like adults. Understanding this will save you a great deal of frustration. Your child still needs a lot of patient teaching and encouragement that is developmentally appropriate. While children of all ages need the opportunity to develop life skills, for preschoolers they are particularly important as life skills form the foundation for healthy self-confidence and self-esteem.

Young children are capable of much more than parents often think, and can be valuable helpers and problem-solvers. Inviting cooperation also can defuse the power struggles over the daily routines that so often afflict families with young children. (For more information on development and parenting for children from ages three to six, see *Positive Discipline for Preschoolers*, Revised Third Edition, Nelsen, Erwin, and Duffy, Three Rivers Press, 2008.)

The School Years

Most parents insist they will celebrate when their children go off to school on that first September morning—and most parents find themselves misty-eyed when they realize that their beloved child is truly moving into a larger world. Regardless of how you choose to educate your child (a subject we will examine more closely in Chapter 12), the school years are busy ones, filled with friends, sports, activities, learning, and a developing knowledge of God and what it means to serve Him.

A normal part of growing up for your child is the increasingly important role that friends will play. Peers are a powerful influence—often a good one, incidentally, rather than a dangerous one. The need children feel to belong and be significant moves into the classroom and church, and, perhaps, onto the athletic field. A wise parent learns his child's unique gifts (and his weaknesses), and helps that child find his special place in his world (more about that in a page or two).

Early Adolescence

We call the years from about 9 to 12 "pre-adolescence"—and these years almost always catch parents off guard. Most parents assume they have until the teen years—13 and up—to deal with adolescence. These parents are in for a bit of a surprise.

For reasons we don't entirely understand, puberty is beginning years earlier now than it ever has before. Girls can begin to menstruate as early as nine years of age; both boys and girls can experience the impact of those delightful things called "hormones" while they're still in elementary school. By middle school the process is in full swing, much to the consternation of everyone involved (including the child).

Many parents believe that as children grow older they need less parenting. The truth is, though, that they need more: they just need it in a different form. They still need kind, firm teaching, time to talk and to be listened to, and a sense of belonging and significance. The more involved they are, the more belonging and significance they will feel and the more effective discipline will be. Throughout this book, we provide examples of ways to get children involved in problem-solving, creating routines, and participating in family meetings because when they are involved in the process of discipline, they are motivated to cooperate.

Of course, Christian parents have lots of help through church involvement. And you'll be happy to know that research shows that children who attend church regularly and who are active in church programs during the eighth grade have higher self-esteem, and are less likely to indulge in risky behaviors. These are years when it is crucial to remain connected and close to your child.

Adolescence

Every parent knows Proverbs 22:6: "Train a child in the way he should go and *when he is old* he will not turn from it." Notice the phrase "when he is old": children who have been well taught (i.e., well-*disciplined*) have solid values planted deep in their hearts. Still, adolescence (*before* they are "old") is a time when many conscientious and loving young people may question what they have been taught in their search for their own individuality and identity. They also do not yet have an adult ability to exercise judgment, set priorities, and weigh risks because the prefrontal cortex of their brains is not yet fully developed (one reason why the leading cause of death in adolescents is accidents and risky behavior). This is, after all, the developmental task of adolescence: your child must become an independent, confident, responsible adult. The process is a complex and often confusing one for both parents and children.

We simply do not believe that the teen years must be filled with rebellion and defiance; teenagers are marvelous people, idealistic, enthusiastic, and bright. In fact, young people can be an example to older ones, as Paul noted when he wrote, "Don't let anyone look down on you because you are young, but set an example for the believers in speech, in life, in love, in faith, and in purity." (1 Timothy 4:12) Many parents, unfortunately, do not understand development well enough to know how best to work with their teen through these years. They sometimes fear the worst and become excessively controlling in an effort to "protect" their teen. Teens react by pulling away. Knowing your child (and the adult he or she is becoming) will help you keep the bond of trust, know how many privileges to grant, and set appropriate limits *with* your teens. (For more information on parenting teenagers, see *Positive Discipline for Teenagers, Revised Second Edition*; Nelsen and Lott; Three Rivers Press; 2000.)

Understanding your child's development, no matter what his or her age, is a critically important way to know who that child is at every stage of his life, and to discover effective ways both to build relationship and to guide behavior.

Spend "Special Time"

Time and money are the two things most adults say they don't have enough of. Of the two, time is certainly the most critical. Take a moment and get a piece of paper and a pencil; now find a quiet spot to think. Make a list of your most important priorities, the things that matter most to you in your life. Most parents list their relationship with God, their partner, and their children near the top (if not first) on the list.

Now make a second list. On this list, write down all the things you actually spend time on each day during the week. Most adults find they spend hours at work, driving, running errands, doing housework, fulfilling obligations to church or school, watching television, and dealing with the thousand-and-one tasks of keeping a family running. Most are shocked to realize how little time they actually spend on their number-one priorities. In fact, a well-known study in the 1970s measured the time fathers spend with their one-year-old children. These fathers claimed to spend 15 to 20 minutes per day with their young children. When the researchers taped the amount of interaction, however, they discovered that the actual time these fathers spent talking and being with their children was 37 seconds per day! (*Seven Promises of a Promise Keeper*, ed. by Janssen and Weeden, Focus on the Family, 1994, p. 116.)

> Knowing your child (and the adult he or she is becoming) will help you keep the bond of trust, know how many privileges to grant, and set appropriate limits with your teens.

In even the most loving and committed of families the American "rat race" is taking its toll. Parents work, and chores must be done. There are church activities and services, and dance, gymnastics, and sports for the kids. Homework and school take up time, too, and technology (computers, smart phones, texting, and video games) are increasingly intrusive. It's not hard to see how parents can find themselves trying to listen, to talk, and to truly understand in 37 seconds a day. And it's just not enough. As Dr. Anthony Witham once said, "Children spell 'love' T-I-M-E."

As you will learn in Chapter 7, one of the reasons children sometimes misbehave is because they equate *attention* with a sense of belonging and significance—a fairly logical opinion from a child's perspective. Parents can both prevent a great deal of misbehavior and build a solid relationship with their children by choosing to make *special time* a priority.

Special time is one-on-one time that you set aside to spend with each child in your family.

It need not be hours; in fact, ten or fifteen minutes on a regular basis may be enough. And you need not spend money on elaborate activities or entertainment. Special time is spent working together, reading or playing together, listening, or just "hanging out." The gift of your time is almost always the best way to tell a child "you matter to me; you belong."

There are many ways of planning special time. You may want to create a "special time calendar" to help you build these precious moments with mom and dad into the week (remember, time is a lot like money: if you don't budget it wisely, it disappears). Some parents take each child in turn to run errands and shop; others plan a "Friday lunch date" with one child each week. However you do it, creating special time with each child will make a big difference in the way your family feels to everyone in it.

Remember, too, that your marriage and your own health and emotional well-being are worth an investment of your time and energy—they are the foundation on which your relationships with your children rest. Take time to nurture yourself in ways that encourage and refresh you, particularly if you are a single parent. If you are married, be sure to keep that relationship strong. It is a huge influence on what your children are learning about life, love, and belonging.

Choose Curiosity Over Judgment

Kim and Mark were settling down to watch a video when their 17-year-old daughter Abigail bounded into the room. "Mom! Dad! It's *so* exciting!" she bubbled. "Just wait 'til you hear!"

"Whoa, Abby," Mark said with a grin. "Settle down and tell us what's going on."

Abigail forced herself to take a deep breath. "The youth group at the fellowship is going to Guatemala this summer! And I'm going, too! It will cost about $1,000, so I'll use my savings and work to repay the money this summer when I get back. Sarah and Christy are going too, and Ryan and Matt. Oh, it will be fabulous! We're going to help build a church and teach the children! You know how it says in the Bible to 'go and make disciples of all nations?' Well, I'm going to *do* it!"

Kim had sat quietly, her face becoming more sober with each word Abigail spoke. She, Mark, and Abigail had always attended a quiet Methodist church, but a few months ago Abigail had gone to a youth rally with friends and had been "born again." Nothing had been the same since. Kim and Mark had allowed her to attend her friends' more active church; Abby enjoyed the upbeat music and energetic youth programs. Her parents had spoken to the youth pastor and met several of the other families. But this was just too much, too soon for Kim.

> Showing genuine curiosity does not mean that you give in to your child's wishes or agree with everything he thinks, feels, or wants. It does mean that your child can learn to trust you with his innermost dreams and hopes.

"Well, you just can't go flying off to South America or somewhere just like that!" she said sourly, realizing that it was probably the first time she'd cut her daughter off while Abby was reciting Scripture. "We don't know these people. And you shouldn't spend your savings on something like this. Besides," she finished lamely, "you haven't had shots. And you don't speak Spanish."

For the first time since she'd entered the room, Abby's enthusiasm dimmed. "Guatemala's in Central America," she said sullenly. "I *knew* you'd be like this! You never want me to do anything!" Abigail burst into tears and ran down the hall to her room, giving the door a vigorous slam behind her.

Mark and Kim looked at each other. "I guess I didn't handle that very well," Kim sighed. "But I just don't feel comfortable with this! It isn't my style, and we *don't* know any of these people very well. How do we know she'll be properly supervised? What if she catches some sort of disease?"

Mark was quiet for a moment. "Well," he said, "we've always raised her to have strong values and to stand up for what she believes. I think we owe it to Abby to hear her out."

The next day, when everyone had cooled off, Mark, Kim, and Abigail sat down together for a family meeting. Mark and Kim had decided to approach Abby with genuine curiosity rather than criticism and judgment. Mark began, "Abby, you caught us a bit off guard last night with this Guatemala trip. This is all pretty new for us, and it's our job to be sure you're safe." Abby rolled her eyes dramatically, a gesture Mark chose to ignore. He continued, "We really want to understand what's going on for you with this trip. We promise to listen without criticizing you, if you'll let us know why this is so important to you."

Abby looked dubious, but she began speaking quietly (after first apologizing for losing her temper the night before). Her new church made this trip every summer, she said, and two of her friends had gone last year. It had been a marvelous experience, one she wanted to share. Abby looked at each of her parents for a moment, then sighed.

"I know you guys worry about me," she said. "But I really think this is okay. I was thinking last night, after I got so mad, about ways I could help you feel better about it. You can call some of the other parents, and you can call the pastors who are going on the trip. You could probably even call the church in Guatemala. And I will repay my savings money. I know I'm supposed to be saving it for college. I'll keep my promise about that. "

Kim smiled slowly. "You *have* been doing some thinking," she said. "I appreciate that you understand why we get worried sometimes. But honey, what makes this trip so important to you?"

Abby sat quietly for a moment before answering. When she looked up, the light in her eyes brought tears to those of her parents. "You always raised me to love God and to want to share His love with others. Now I have a chance to do something *real*, something more than just putting my dollar in the offering plate on Sunday. And I want to make a difference in the world. I want to help someone else, because I have so much."

Kim didn't say a word; she just reached over and hugged her daughter. There would be a lot of work to do in the months ahead. Kim and Mark did make many calls, but eventually they decided that while it was hard to let Abby fly away, she would be well cared-for and would have a priceless opportunity to learn and grow. They decided to split the cost of the trip with her. And they also discovered that curiosity and a willingness to really *listen* opened their daughter's heart, while judgment and criticism closed it tight.

Showing genuine curiosity does not mean that you give in to your child's wishes or agree with everything he thinks, feels, or wants. It *does* mean that your child can learn to trust you with his innermost dreams and hopes. And it will help you set limits, when necessary, that work for you and for your child because those limits are based on a full understanding of the issues at hand. Curiosity—genuine interest in who your child is becoming—is one of the surest ways to get into his world and understand him.

Be Aware of the Influence of Technology and Culture

Your child may go to a church-related school, or be schooled at home. You may attend church services regularly and monitor your child's friends and activities. Still, our mass media and culture have never been as pervasive as they are right now, and when lack of connection and belonging in a family creates a void, the culture—the media, advertising, television, social networking, and music so prevalent in our society—will rush in to fill it. Christian families, sad to say, are not immune.

Exodus 23:2 tells us, "Do not follow the crowd in doing wrong." Wise words: but wise parents must be aware of just how large the crowd is, and where it is going. Technology has become a part of everyday family life. We are surrounded by DVD players, smart phones, MP3 players, iPads, computers, and even the Nook or Kindle. Some schools require students to own and use a computer. Technology is not dangerous in and of itself; it can hold wonderful benefits. But there are risks. Many children and teens spend hours "surfing the 'Net," chatting on social network sites, or texting, often in their rooms alone, while time for family meetings and conversation is rare. And it is not only the children who are addicted: many parents, too, spend hours on technology, hours that could be spent connecting with children and partners.

Television in particular poses risks to children. How many of you would intentionally invite into your home on a daily basis people who promote violence, incivility, and sexual immorality to your children? In effect, isn't that what we do when we allow our children to watch prime-time television indiscriminately? Some of the risks of television are obvious: "Little House on the Prairie" and "Father Knows Best" are long gone, replaced by prime-time television filled with sexual innuendo and violence. Even the evening news can provide an education on subjects most parents would rather their children avoid.

Some of the risks television poses, however, are less apparent. Watching television is an entirely passive activity: it does not teach language and is not as educational as most parents assume. Television before bedtime can disrupt sleep patterns and make getting children to bed more difficult. Young children cannot differentiate between reality and fantasy, and may be willing targets for the billions of dollars in advertising directed at them (and at their parents' wallets). Children do not learn to use critical thinking skills while watching. Remember, we don't call it "the boob tube" for nothing!

It isn't necessary to take your television to the dump (even though it might be a good idea). But it is wise to restrict the amount of time your children spend in front of it. In fact, the American Association of Pediatrics recommends no television at all (yes, you heard us correctly) for children under the age of two. Some research indicates that too much screen time (TV or computers) before the age of eight can be harmful to optimal brain development.

If your children do watch television in your home (and there is a great deal of valuable programming available), it is wise to watch it *with* them. Ask "what" and "how" questions to learn what they are thinking; ask them what they would do if they found themselves in the situations portrayed on TV. And if you have a computer, consider placing it in a common space in your home (the living room or family study, for instance). Teach your children about Internet safety.

> Some research indicates that too much screen time (TV or computers) before the age of eight can be harmful to optimal brain development.

Like money, technology is a tool. It can be used for good or it can be used for evil. You must determine the role culture and technology will play in your home, but showing curiosity and listening well will keep you connected to your children, who often move in a wider world than their parents suppose. It is rarely possible to control every influence your child encounters, and it may not even be wise to try. Putting certain music or friends off-limits, for example, often makes them unbearably attractive to young people, and unless you can watch your child 24 hours a day, you may be setting up unnecessary power struggles. Consider using curiosity questions and respectful discussion to set limits *with* your child's cooperation.

After all, children must learn to live in a real world with real challenges, without being "conformed to this world." By confronting these challenges together, and taking time to stay connected, you and your children can thrive, and can be "transformed by the renewing of your mind. Then you will be able to test and approve what God's will is—his good, pleasing, and perfect will." (Romans 12:2)

Share Your Own History

Try this little experiment: ask your child what he or she thinks you do all day long, where you grew up, or what your favorite activity was. The answers you get may surprise you.

Children frequently know very little about their parents as *people*. And sharing your own history, dreams, and experiences can be a wonderful way to connect with your child. Here are some suggestions:

- Get out your old scrapbooks and photo albums, and share memories and stories about your own childhood, adolescence, and young adulthood. Let your children laugh at your adventures, but don't be afraid to share painful memories and mistakes as well. Sometimes children draw closer to parents when they realize their parents are human, and as susceptible to hurt and longing as they are.
- Invite your children to interview a family member, perhaps a parent, an aunt or uncle, or a grandparent. Children love to hear about their parents' escapades as children (especially the times when they misbehaved). One grandfather told his grandchildren a story each time they visited about "Nip on the Joystick," tales about a cat named Nip who was a pilot during World War II. Not surprisingly, these stories were based on that grandfather's own experiences, and even the older children looked forward to hearing them. You can share what you learn about each other at a family meeting.
- Take your child to work with you for a day. Most children love to explore a parent's workplace, and it helps them understand what life is like for you—including the reasons you may need time to relax at the end of a busy day!
- Share your hobbies and interests with your children. Take them to performances and museums; let them work on car engines or motorcycles with you. Whatever you love, share that thing with your children.

Your own imagination and creativity will give you other ideas. Sharing your *self* with those you love is a powerful way to build bridges between you.

Build a Spiritual Life Together

"Hear, O Israel: The Lord our God, the Lord is one. Love the Lord your God with all your heart and with all your soul and with all your strength. These commandments that I give you today are to be upon your hearts. Impress them on your children. Talk about them when you sit at home and when you walk along the road, when you lie down and when you get up. Tie them as symbols on your hands and bind them on your foreheads. Write them on the doorframes of your houses and on your gates."

(Deuteronomy 6:4-9)

Has there ever been a more powerful exhortation to parents to share their faith than these this? Our love of God is to be written on the doorframes of our homes; it is to be a part of our daily conversation. One way for Christian families to connect with each other is to make their faith a living part of each and every day they spend together. Faith is always more than just the words we speak. As James wrote, "Faith without works is dead." (James 2:20) Our beliefs must be part of the very fabric of our lives with our children. Here are some suggestions for creating a spiritual life your family can share, one that reaches beyond Sunday worship service:

- Invite each child to take turns beginning your family meetings with a prayer, a Scripture, or a song.
- Discover ways your family can work together to make your community a better place. You might "adopt" a family for the holidays, work to clean up a park, or spend time working in your local food bank or homeless shelter. Invite your children to choose ways they can put "legs" on their faith.
- Ask for your children's prayers. When you make a mistake, lose your temper, or are struggling with a problem, ask your children to help you by praying with you, and for you. What a marvelous way to teach them that they can influence their world and offer support to their parents!
- Make mistakes real opportunities to learn. You may decide that when anyone in the family makes a mistake or is disrespectful, that person can choose to put a dime in the family "faith jar." When the jar is full, you can decide together how to use the money. Perhaps you can buy a present for a needy child, donate blankets to a homeless shelter, or give to a favorite church program. Imagine how much better mistakes will feel when you can use them to help someone else!

Each of your children must eventually learn to hold onto his faith in a difficult and challenging world. But creating a solid foundation of shared love and belief will help "train them up in the way they should go."

Love Your Children Enough To Let Them Go

Did you know that loving parents are a lot like eagles? In Deuteronomy 32:11, we see a picture of an eagle that "stirs up its nest and hovers over its young, that spreads its wings to catch them and carries them on its pinions." In other words, the eagle makes it clear her young cannot stay in the nest forever, but she lets go gradually, supporting, teaching, and encouraging her babies along the way.

Letting go may seem like an odd way to build connection and to get into your child's world. But in some ways, parenting is *all* about letting go, from the moment your child begins to take her first wobbly steps, to her first day of school, to the day she leaves your home for her husband's. Loving parents learn that one of the best ways to create trust, understanding, and lifelong love is to let go in appropriate ways at appropriate times.

When parents cannot let go, children often resort to pushing them away. The resulting power struggles, hurt feelings, and grief are painful for everyone. Letting go is painful for parents—but it is necessary.

In her book , *Loving and Letting Go* (Zondervan, 2000), Carol Kuykendall, former director of communications for Mothers of Preschoolers International, describes her own experiences:

"From the moment I became a mother, I began a process of transformation that is still changing who I am. Since the births of each of our three children, I've been filled with a growing, powerful mother love that affects the way I think and act. It both fills me to bursting and drains me to emptiness. It both confuses and consumes me. It brings out my best and my worst. It often tangles me up and keeps me from carrying out the right decision, even when I know what the right decision is. Mother love grips my heart and gets in the way of letting go, which is often the hardest part of parenting.

Yet the older I get, and the older my children get, the more I realize how God uses our children—as he uses all our life experiences—to teach us his most profound lessons, especially about this challenge of loving and letting go, which applies to all of life." (p. 13)

Loving children means teaching them well, loving them unconditionally, encouraging them daily, and letting go day by day as they begin their journeys toward their own destiny. Letting go is rarely easy, but it is essential. Being willing to do so tells your children more surely than any words that you have faith in them and trust their ability to make good choices. And it ensures that they will return again and again to enjoy the relationship of respect, closeness, and trust that they have built with you.

GETTING INTO YOUR CHILD'S WORLD

- Understand development and developmental appropriateness

- Spend special time

- Choose curiosity over judgment

- Be aware of the influence of technology and culture

- Share your own history

- Build a spiritual life together

- Love your children enough to let go

Chapter 6

What Does Birth Order Have to Do With This?

"The boys grew up, and Esau became a skillful hunter, a man of the open country, while Jacob was a quiet man, staying among the tents."

(Genesis 25:27)

The Rhodes children, ages eleven, nine, and six, are as different from one another as any three children chosen at random. At least, that's what their parents will tell you. Maria, eleven going on twenty-nine, is Miss Organizer. Her room is neat as a pin, her school books and notebooks are all color-coded, and she insists on doing all her own wash lest it somehow get mixed up with that of her brother and sister. She's an overachiever in school, sports, and her music lessons, and she tends to be a bit bossy. Maria, says her brother, needs to "get a life."

Sarah, the nine-year-old, is everything Maria is not. Sociable, fun loving, always on the go, Sarah plays a different role in school, sports, and music. Counterpoint to Maria, Sarah frequently gets in trouble for talking in school, for goofing off during soccer practice, and for playing tricks on her piano teacher. Sarah has too much of a life.

Josh, the only boy, is the baby—in more ways than one. Blessed (or cursed) with three "moms," he is doted on, waited on, fawned over, and treated more like a family mascot than a child. He is learning how to make the best of getting everyone else to take care of him. For Josh, this IS the life!

Jonas Salk gave us the memorable prescription for good parenting. Good parents, he said, give their children roots and wings. Wise mothers and fathers know that children need roots so they'll always know where home is and where their values come from, and wings so they can test what they learned on their own, making their own mistakes and learning from them. As the Scripture suggests, Esau represented wings and Jacob was roots. Esau was "a skillful hunter," a man of action, extroverted, hands-on, always seeking new adventure. Jacob, on the other hand, was "a quiet man, who stayed among the tents," a man whose highest values were hearth and home, a family man, a contented man. Two brothers with the same parents, but very different indeed. Have you experienced that in your own family?

While it isn't the entire explanation, birth order has a lot to do with the roles your children choose in life. It is no accident that Maria, for example, is a high achiever who tends to be a bit bossy. In that respect, she has more in common with firstborn children all over the world than she does with her own siblings. And Sarah's assumption of a very different role from Maria's is no accident either; Maria had already defined her role in the family, so Sarah, pursuing her own way to belong and find significance (remember the primary human need?), carved out a very different role for herself. And Josh—well, he's the baby. His role is clear, and he will play it for all it's worth. After all, it is certainly working well for him!

The Scriptures are filled with references to sibling differences and sibling rivalries, from the very beginnings with Cain and Abel, Esau and Jacob, and the jealousies of Joseph's brothers, to the prodigal son and his resentful brother in the Gospels. Dr. Kevin Leman, author of *The Birth Order Book: Why You Are the Way You Are* (Revised Updated Edition, Baker Publishing Group, 2009), swears that his recommended title for that book was *Abel Had It Coming*, a comical reference to the role of birth order in sibling rivalry. Those of us with two children can easily imagine the scenario: Cain was in his room studying for his spelling test when little Abel sneaked in, threw a dirty sock at him, giggled triumphantly, and ran away. Cain chased after him and bopped him on the head. Abel cried out, "M-o-o-m, Cain hit me!" Eve yelled at Cain for not acting his age, and Cain flipped out. And therein lies the problem.

Of course, we don't know that Eve yelled at Cain, "You are the oldest, and you should know better," but we know this is a common occurrence in many homes. Taking the side of one child over another creates a family atmosphere of competition that increases differences.

> Taking the side of one child over another creates a family atmosphere of competition that increases differences.

Competition between children also is encouraged when parents disagree on how to parent. Even when parents have similar parenting strategies, children still choose different slices of the "family pie" as they seek their individual perceptions of how to find belonging and significance in their families.

Birth order is not the only factor that determines children's personalities and the roles they assume in their families. Most parents have heard of the debate over "nature versus nurture." Is it genes— the gifts, traits, and abilities God gives each new human being—that determine who that person becomes, or is the environment they are raised in—including the choices their parents make about discipline, teaching, and nurturing—the more powerful factor? It has even been suggested that parents have little to do with the adults their children become: according to Judith Rich Harris (*The Nurture Assumption: Why Children Turn Out the Way They Do, Revised and Updated, Free Press, 2009*), only genes and the influence of their peers influence children's personalities. (A theory the authors of this book do not believe, incidentally, and that has been widely discredited.)

We believe, along with many other researchers and professionals who study human behavior, that both genes and environment are important, but there is yet another factor, perhaps the most powerful of all. Each person, from the time he is very young, watches what goes on around him. He has thoughts and perceptions about what he experiences; he has feelings. And he makes decisions about what it all means, what he must do to find belonging and significance, what he must do to survive or thrive in his family. Perhaps this powerful part of human nature is what has been called our "soul" or our "spirit"; in any case, it often means that what happens to us is less important than what we *decide* about what happens to us. As we have seen, Maria, Sarah, and Josh all made different decisions about their place in their family and the way they would find belonging. An understanding of birth order can increase our understanding of how our children might develop misperceptions about themselves based on their interpretations of their place in the family.

Birth order helps us understand the belief behind the behavior, the "why" behind the "what." As we have seen, children—and adults, for that matter—are always making decisions and forming beliefs about themselves, others, and the world based on their life experiences. Their behavior is then based upon those decisions and what they believe they need to do to find a sense of belonging and worth. It is very common for children to compare themselves to their siblings and decide that if a brother or sister is doing well in a certain area, then their only choice must be one of the following:

- to develop competence in a completely different area;
- to compete and try to be better than the sibling;
- to be rebellious or revengeful; and/or
- to give up due to the mistaken belief that they can't compete with the sibling.

The Parts We Play

Being in a family is like being in a play, with each birth order position representing one part and with each part having distinct and separate characteristics. If one sibling has already filled a part, such as "the good child," other siblings may feel that they have to find other parts to play, such as the rebellious child, the academic child, the athletic child, the family clown, and so on.

> ...*what happens to us is less important than what we decide about what happens to us.*

Children who have the same birth order position often have surprising similarities, even though they come from different families with different values and rules. From the perspective of family values, children from one family may tend to be quite similar (and even excel in the same areas) when the family atmosphere is one of cooperation.

Even though their personalities and behavior appear to be different, Maria, Sarah, and Josh Rhodes are all developing the family values and belief system of their parents. The challenge to Mr. and Mrs. Rhodes is not whether their children will adopt their beliefs, but how their self-image will develop and how they will learn to deal with others. It is in these critical areas—self-esteem and relationship skills—that understanding birth order can have the greatest positive effect.

Will Maria's leadership tendencies result in her becoming an effective and respected motivator of people, or a demanding, overly critical authoritarian? Will Sarah's sociable and playful nature lead her to become a positive and supportive encourager of people, or a frivolous young woman who has difficulty seeing the serious side of life? Will Josh's role as recipient of his family's caring and concern lead to his becoming an empathic, caring person who reaches out to people in need, or an irresponsible slacker who expects the world to take care of him?

Children in the same family are usually quite different, even though they have the same parents, the same family values, the same home, and the same neighborhood. Of course, the environment cannot be totally the same for each child in the family—we are not the same parents of our third child that we were of our first. We probably expected more of our first than we did of our third, and we probably paid more attention to that firstborn as well. (After all, three children take up considerably more time and energy than does just one!) But the factor that makes the biggest contribution to differences within families is the interpretation each child gives to his place in the environment.

Children tend to view themselves differently depending upon their birth order position. Firstborns tend to see themselves very seriously as they move through life having every accomplishment—first tooth, first words, first steps—duly celebrated by their parents. The parents, in turn, tend to see their firstborn child as a reflection of themselves, and a perfect little reflection at that. "Do us proud" is often the message that the firstborn hears from the parent.

Second-born children may enter this family of father, mother, and perfect little firstborn and conclude that they can't possibly live up to the image of their older sibling and, therefore, need to carve out a different role, perhaps the role of troublemaker. Middle-born children are often confused about their identity. They are not at the top of the heap, expected to assume the role of leader; nor are they at the bottom, allowed to live out the role of pampered baby. Unsure of how they fit into the family constellation, middle-born children often look outside the family for relationships. As a result, they tend to be the most comfortably sociable of the children.

As we saw in the previous chapter, children are good perceivers but poor interpreters. This becomes apparent in the study of birth order. The truth of a situation is not as important as each person's interpretation of a situation, and behavior is based on the latter. Children of the same birth order often make similar interpretations about themselves and how they think they need to behave in order to find belonging and significance in life.

A Case Study: Maria, Sarah, and Josh

Let's use our opening story of Maria, Sarah, and Josh to help us better understand how birth order fits into the parenting puzzle. The most predictable similarities are found among oldest children, because this is the one position that has the fewest variables. There are many ways to be a middle child, such as the middle of three or one of the middles of seven. As for only children, they will be more similar to oldest or youngest, depending on whether they were pampered like a youngest or given more responsibility like an oldest. And youngest children have almost as many predictable similarities as do oldest children.

Maria, the firstborn, is the little adult. As she grows and develops, she has two people to look to as models, Mom and Dad. They are caring, loving, and mature, and Maria does her best to follow their example. In so doing, she may walk early and talk early, and her vocabulary may be quite advanced. (After all, she's spending all her time talking to grown-ups!) She may try hard to do the right thing, be polite with all the adults in her life, and get good grades in school. Mom and Dad will proudly take her to church, to the grocery store, to the mall, and to friends' and relatives' homes because she is so well behaved.

As a firstborn, she may become a member of a very special group, the overachievers. She has a lot of company. In *The New Birth Order Book,* Dr. Kevin Leman relates the following statistics about firstborns:

- Of the first twenty-three astronauts sent into outer space, twenty-one were firstborns (Neil Armstrong, the first man to walk on the moon, was, of course, a firstborn).
- All seven astronauts in the original Mercury program were firstborns.
- More than half the United States presidents were firstborns.
- Firstborns are over-represented among *Who's Who in America* and *American Men and Women of Science,* as well as among Rhodes scholars and university professors.
- Firstborns tend to be highly motivated to achieve. They tend to be analytical, organized, and precise, and they thrive on structure and order.

Firstborns tend to be highly motivated to achieve. They tend to be analytical, organized, and precise, and they thrive on structure and order.

The firstborn child is likely to spend hours sorting baseball cards, meticulously furnishing a doll house, playing school (with the firstborn being the teacher and her friends or siblings being relegated to the role of the students), or strategically positioning the latest action figures around the room. When Mary and Joseph found Jesus in the temple, "sitting in the midst of the teachers, listening to them and asking them questions," he was behaving with the maturity of a classic firstborn. The only child tends to become either a super lastborn or a super firstborn, depending on his parents' expectations of him.

The bottom line is that Children tend to develop according to the perception they have of their parents' expectations and treatment of them and/or their older siblings' expectations and treatment of them. And birth order is a major factor in those expectations and treatment. Maria will get a lot of adult attention, and because she is the firstborn, a lot will be expected of her. The firstborn perceives this and responds accordingly.

Interestingly enough, some firstborns don't care for their position and the expectations that go along with it and become the family rebels. It is important to remember that you cannot predict a child's personality or behavior from birth order alone. Theories on human behavior are meant to help us better understand what we see and hear, rather than become obstacles for preconceived judgment and unearned labels.

The second born, particularly if she is of the same gender as the firstborn, may develop the belief that she needs to do something different from the firstborn to experience belonging and significance in the family. Even though the parents have the same rules and expectations for both children, the second born tends to perceive something very different. Many parents think it is an effective discipline tool to compare children: "Why can't you be more like your sister?" However, comparisons are usually perceived as extremely hurtful and discouraging to children and they often react by rebelling or becoming vengeful to hurt back. ("It hurts when you love me conditionally, so I'll get even by *not* living up to your expectations—even if hurting you hurts me too in the long run.")

If Sarah is to achieve significance in her family, she will need to find it somewhere other than the places Maria found it. Her first tooth, step, words, smile, and drawings may be far less significant than her older sister's. So she must look for another way to be noticed, and second-born children sometimes find it in rebellion. If the firstborn was "Mr. Do-Whatever-Mom-and-Dad-Want" (because they will clap and celebrate and call all the aunts and uncles when he does), then the second-born may try to do whatever Mom and Dad don't want. After all, doing whatever Mom and Dad want is no longer any big deal—the firstborn already took care of that. (Learning to encourage your children, to truly connect with them, and to listen well to both their words and their behavior can help you guide your children towards positive behavior and roles. We will learn more about these skills in the chapters ahead.)

Just as Sarah began to sort out her place in the family, along came Josh. Josh's entry into the family does not make matters any easier for Sarah. Not only does she not get the attention of the firstborn (except the negative attention she's been receiving for her "naughtiness"), now there's a new baby—and a boy at that—to further distract attention from her. She's literally being squeezed in the middle, between two siblings with clear roles to play in the family. It would be easy for her to decide, "Mommy loves that baby more than me. I'll have to try harder to win her back." Sometimes trying harder means acting like a baby; other times an older child may try to be better than the new sibling, even talking for them to show her own superiority.

It's fair to ask what Josh will learn from his childhood experiences as a last-born. Will he learn manipulation, and to expect special service? Or will he learn empathy and caring from the empathy he received from his parents and sisters? His experiences, and the decisions he makes about them, will shape the man he becomes.

Same, But Different

All oldest children will not form the exact same conclusions and be exactly alike, nor will all middle children, all only children, or all youngest children. Each human being is a unique creation, but those of the same birth order often adopt similar characteristics. Before you read further, close your eyes and think of several adjectives that come to your mind to describe the oldest, youngest, and middle children you know. We will discuss the similarities first, the variables that account for uniqueness, and finally the exceptions to the general rules.

It is easy to come up with descriptions of oldest children, such as *responsible, leader, bossy, perfectionist, critical* (of self and others), *conformist, organized, competitive, independent, reluctant risk-takers,* or *conservative.* Because oldest children are the firstborn, they often adopt the mistaken interpretation that they must be first or best in order to be important. This can be manifested in many different ways. For some it may seem important to get their schoolwork done first, even though it is sloppy. Others may be the last to hand in their work because they take so much time making it the best. As we've seen, Maria fits this picture perfectly.

The characteristic most people think of first to describe youngest children is "spoiled." Many youngest children are pampered, both by parents and by other siblings. This makes it very easy for them to adopt the mistaken interpretation that they must continue to manipulate others into their service in order to be important. Youngest children are often skilled in using their charm to inspire others to do things for them and can be creative and fun-loving. Much of their creativity, energy, and intelligence may be channeled into achieving significance through charming manipulation. Josh is becoming a master of this.

Some youngest children are put in the confusing position of being favored by parents and resented by their siblings. The story of Joseph is an excellent example of this. "Now Israel loved Joseph more than any of his other sons . . . When his brothers saw that their father loved him more than any of them, they hated him and could not even speak a kind word to him." (Genesis 37: 3-4) Favoritism is as hurtful as comparisons, and often results in revenge. The brothers' hatred and jealousy was so strong that they decided to kill Joseph, an act that was thwarted by one brother, Reuben, the firstborn, who, typical of firstborns, was overcome by a sense of responsibility.

The greatest danger for children who have been pampered is that they often interpret life as unfair whenever they are not taken care of or given whatever they want. They may think they have a right to have temper tantrums, feel sorry for themselves, or seek revenge in some way that is destructive or hurtful to others when their expectations are not met. Joseph was put in an environment where he was no longer pampered or favored. He developed great character and many skills, and one day was given the opportunity to save his family from starvation.

Youngest children may have difficulty adjusting to school. They may feel not only that the teacher should continue the service they have received at home but that the teacher should also learn for them. Consciously they say, "Teacher, please tie my shoes for me." Subconsciously, and by their actions, they are saying, "And while you are at it, please learn for me." "I can't" and "show me" are often simple demands to "do it for me."

"Who Dresses You in the Morning?"

During her years as an elementary school counselor, Jane Nelsen talked with many children who were struggling at school. She learned to ask these children a telling question: "Who dresses you in the morning?" As you might guess, children who have trouble in school often have someone else taking care of them, sometimes long past the time when they have developed the ability (and the need) to take care of themselves. The result is a discouraged child.

Children can dress themselves from the time they are two years old if they have clothes that are easy to put on and have been taught how to do it. When parents continue to dress their children (or wait on them) when they are able to do things for themselves, they are robbing them of opportunities to experience and learn responsibility, self-sufficiency, and self-confidence—to develop the belief "I am capable." Without these skills, they will not be good learners in school, nor will they develop the skills they need for success in life.

> *Take time for training, and then allow children to develop responsibility and self-confidence.*

Since pampering is damaging to children, why do parents do it? Many parents really believe they are showing love to their children. These parents are not aware of how difficult it is to change beliefs, habits, and characteristics once they are established. Unfortunately, the well-known advice in Proverbs 22:6 ("Train a child in the way he should go; even when he is old, he will not turn from it.") can work both ways.

Parents are not really thinking about the long-range effects when they rob their children of the opportunity to practice life skills because parents can do it easier, faster, and better. The parents who say they "just don't have time" to let children do things for themselves may later be disappointed and frustrated when they discover their children didn't develop the life skills and attitudes needed by a capable, confident adult. Parents who want the best for their children may need to re-evaluate their time priorities, no longer doing *for* children. Effective parents slow down to be sure that children learning valuable life skills are afforded the time they need.

Take time for training, and then allow children to develop responsibility and self-confidence. It is a mistake to think children can always learn to take care of themselves later. The longer they wait, the more difficult it is to change their interpretations of how life is and what they think they need to do to find belonging and significance.

Many youngest children choose an entirely different interpretation of life and become "speeders." They often adopt the mistaken interpretation that they must catch up with and outdo everyone ahead of them in order to be important. They become adults who are overachievers still trying to prove their significance.

It is more difficult to generalize about the characteristics of middle children because of their many different positions. They usually feel squeezed in the middle, without the privileges of the oldest or the benefits of the youngest. They may adopt the mistaken belief that they must be different in some way in order to be significant. Middle children may overachieve or underachieve, becoming a "social butterfly," a "wallflower," or a rebel—with or without a cause. Many are more easygoing than their siblings. Most middle children have a great deal of empathy for the underdog, with whom they identify. They are often good peacemakers, and others seek them out for sympathy and understanding. They are usually much more open-minded than the oldest, more conservative sibling.

Only children may be similar to oldest or youngest children, with some important differences. They may have less desire for perfectionism, because they haven't felt the pressure from siblings to prove their own worth. Still, only children usually have the same high expectations of themselves that they feel from their parents. Because they have been the only child in the family, they usually desire and appreciate solitude—or they may fear loneliness. It may be more important for them to be unique than to be first.

"Somebody Threw Away the Birth Order Rules in My Family!"

Can't figure out where your children and family fit yet? Perhaps you need to consider one or more of the most common variables in the birth order theory. Birth order becomes a bit more complicated when considering multiple births (as in twins, or triplets or more), adoptions, stepfamilies, and other complexities in the more usual family constellation. Today there are more multiple births due to fertility science advances, and this can throw a monkey wrench into the usual interpretations of "who does what." Those most affected by multiple "new babies" is the older sibling, whose bubble experiences a sharp pricking, as he realizes that there is more than one new "ruler" on the parental throne. Thus the struggle for belonging and significance begins again. Twins—and other multiple births—challenge the usual descriptions of birth order.

Some other variables to understanding birth order include the blending of two or more families, the spacing of children, the sex of each child, cognitive, emotional, or physical differences between children, adoptions, sibling deaths, and the birth order positioning of each parent. (For more information on birth order and parenting in stepfamilies, see *Positive Discipline for Your Stepfamily, Revised 2nd Edition,* Nelsen, Erwin, and Glenn, Prima, 2000, available as a download at www.positivediscipline.com.)

Your parenting style is heavily influenced by your own birth order and how you resolved the question of belonging and significance yourself. You bring this past history into the present mix of birth order principles. The birth order of parents not only affects the family atmosphere, it also affects the marriage partnership, and it is helpful for parents to understand how their parenting affects their children as the search for their piece of the puzzle within the family begins. Although each birth order position has general, defining tendencies and specific characteristics common for each of the positions, the key to understanding how birth order functions in any given family comes through understanding the relationships between this family's members.

What Does It All Mean?

How does birth order information help us to understand children, to be more effective parents, and to encourage better behavior? Being aware of a child's birth order, as well as the birth order of each parent, will allow you to make some intelligent guesses about your child's world and point of view, and how you might interact with each other in healthy, effective ways. This awareness will help you understand the importance of not pampering children, providing oldest children with opportunities to feel okay about not always being first, helping middle children feel less squeezed, and understanding the unique world each of your children perceives and lives in. (For more detailed information about birth order, see Chapter 3 in *Positive Discipline, R*evised Updated Edition, Ballantine Books, 2006, or *The Birth Order Book: The Why You Are the Way You Are* (Revised Updated Edition, Baker Publishing Group, 2009.)

> *Your parenting style is heavily influenced by your own birth order and how you resolved the question of belonging and significance yourself.*

Remember, birth order is only one factor in children's personalities and behavior. In families where competition is valued and modeled (as in many American families), differences will be magnified. In families where cooperation is valued and modeled, differences will be decreased and family harmony will increase.

But isn't the competitive spirit a valued American trait? It certainly has value on the athletic field, but we believe that it is far more helpful to children to teach them cooperation, to help them develop the ability to work with others, and to value others' gifts and abilities (even when those "others" are their siblings). Paul gives us a wonderful example of the spirit of appreciation and cooperation in his first letter to the Corinthians:

"There are different kinds of gifts, but the same Spirit. There are different kinds of service, but the same Lord. There are different kinds of working but the same God works all of them in all men. Now to each one the manifestation of the Spirit is given for the common good . . . the message of wisdom; . . . the message of knowledge; . . . faith; . . . gifts of healing; . . . miraculous powers; . . . prophecy; . . .to distinguish between spirits; . . . the ability to speak in different kinds of tongues; . . . interpretation of tongues." (1 Corinthians 12:4-10)

Paul's words remind us that each of us has unique gifts and that each of us belongs in the Body of Christ. Parents and children each belong equally in the family. What a beautiful metaphor this is for the longing we all experience to find belonging. It is possible to find this belonging in our own positive and unique ways—within our own family.

Birth order can teach us a lot about ourselves and others. We use birth order knowledge not to classify or stereotype people, but to better understand why they might do the things they do; we can then try to find ways to encourage them. Paul said in 1 Thessalonians 5:11: "Encourage one another, and build each other up." A knowledge of birth order helps us see more clearly why our children do the things they do and why, when, and how they will need our encouragement.

Chapter 7

The Four Goals of Misbehavior: Why Do Kids Do What They Do?

"All she wants is attention!"
"It seems like we're always fighting."
"I have no idea why he hurts his brother so often!"
"She never listens to me!"

Have you ever heard yourself muttering these and other frustrating complaints as you confront your misbehaving child? All parents recognize that even the "best" children occasionally misbehave, but on those truly difficult days it can seem as though your child's misbehavior is a carefully planned plot to frustrate and defeat you. Although it certainly may seem as though kids misbehave just to make you miserable, Alfred Adler, through his observations of human behavior, realized that children (and most other people) are actually using their misbehavior to tell us something—their misbehavior is a "code."

Sometimes misbehavior occurs for physical reasons, and parents are usually adept at reading these clues. Because children (especially young children) lack articulate language skills, they communicate to the adults around them with their behavior. When children are overtired, over-stimulated, or hungry, parents can easily read their misbehavior as a "code," their way of telling us what they need, such as a nap, a snack, or time to run around outdoors and use up some of that excess energy. This is the origin of the phrase "acting out." This kind of misbehavior is fairly easy to understand (although it always seems to happen when you are least able to respond calmly). But what about the times when there is no obvious explanation for bad behavior? Believe it or not, human behavior *always* has a purpose, whether we understand it or not. In Positive Discipline, we take you beyond the misbehavior to the belief *behind* the behavior.

Alfred Adler and Rudolf Dreikurs presented a whole new way of thinking about human behavior by linking thoughts and feelings to

> *Because children (especially young children) lack articulate language skills, they communicate to the adults around them with their behavior.*

behavior. (Perhaps the idea wasn't completely new: Proverbs 23:7c says, "For as he thinks within himself, so he is.") Adults can help children change their behavior when they learn to "break the code," and understand that what children are really seeking with their misbehavior is a sense of *belonging and significance.* Parents must learn to follow God's own example, looking in the heart for understanding of behavior.

In Positive Discipline workshops, we help participants understand that human misbehavior is more complex than merely "acting out" for attention. (And yes, as you will see, gaining attention is one of the four mistaken goals of misbehavior.) Although it may seem that a child's behavior is *always* a bid for attention, children who misbehave are feeling discouraged and may be attempting to find belonging and connection by using an inappropriate approach.

> Children who misbehave are feeling discouraged and may be attempting to find belonging and connection by using an inappropriate approach.

After all, to a child, an argument with Dad sure *feels* like connection—even if it's a negative one. And because punishment—spanking, grounding, taking away privileges, and lectures—deals only with behavior, it almost never changes the inner beliefs that are motivating that behavior. This is why so many parents claim punishment "works" and yet find that they have to keep punishing their children for the same misbehavior over and over again.

You may be thinking, "Are you kidding? How can a child who whines, acts defiant, refuses to go to church, or hits her brother be seeking belonging and significance?" Perhaps it is easier to see how a child who is *not* misbehaving meets the goal of belonging and significance without resorting to misbehavior.

A child who behaves appropriately gets her goals met in positive ways, as we see in this brief scene in the family kitchen:

Four-year-old Megan shares her warm sugar cookie with her 2-year-old brother, Nathan.

- Megan gets the *attention* she needs from her little brother, who hugs her, and from Mommy, who says, "That was a nice thing to do, Megan."
- Megan is exerting her *power and influence* in a positive way by choosing, all on her own, to share with Nathan.
- Megan feels a wonderful sense of *belonging and significance*, especially when Mommy encourages her kind act by saying with a kiss, "Thank you for sharing with your little brother."

Encouragement is Key to Understanding the Mistaken Goals

Dreikurs once said, "Encouragement is to humans like water is to plants. It nourishes our souls." The Bible agrees: Hebrews 3:13 tells us to "encourage one another daily." Ideally, children meet their need for belonging and significance by behaving in ways that are pleasing and desirable. And they will repeat positive behavior more often when their parents notice and encourage it. Through consistent use of the Positive Discipline tools, Christian parents can help a child stop misbehaving to gain negative attention, experience misguided power, seek revenge, or assume a sense of inadequacy. (More about the specific goals in a moment.) Encouraged children who know they belong have little need to misbehave. (Of course, it's not a perfect system!)

Scripture tells us that we should not "merely listen to the word, and so deceive ourselves. Do what it says. . . . Faith, by itself, if it is not accompanied by action, is dead." (James 1:22; 2:17-18) In Proverbs 20:11, God says, "Even a child is known by his actions, by whether his conduct is pure and right." As we have said, children usually *do* better when they *feel* better, and a child's interpretation of belonging may look very different than an adult's. Let's look at an example.

Remember Megan, the four-year-old girl who shared her cookie with her brother? Well, now it's Sunday morning after church, and Megan is waiting to go home. Mom and Dad are talking with friends. Worse, they're ignoring Megan. When Megan pulls on Mom's dress to get her attention, Mom looks down and says, "Just a moment, Megan," and goes right on talking. Megan is not feeling that she belongs, nor does she feel particularly significant. In fact, she feels cranky, tired, and hungry—and ignored. And she knows just what to do about it. She yanks on Mom's dress again, harder this time. And when Mom tries to ignore her, she pushes Mom and whines in a loud voice that is impossible to ignore, "Mom, I want to go home *now*!"

Embarrassed, Megan's parents end their conversation, give Megan a lecture about manners, and head for the car. Megan may be in trouble, but even trouble is better than being ignored. Megan has demonstrated the mistaken goal of undue attention—and her parents have unwittingly reinforced her behavior by giving in to it.

Parents can unintentionally foster misbehavior by failing to notice and nurture behaviors they value. But like thirsty plants, children need encouragement; receiving it prevents the drought of discouragement—and the misbehavior that so often follows. (More on encouragement in Chapter 9.)

Misbehavior Signals the Beginning of Discouragement

"A misbehaving child is a discouraged child," Dreikurs tells us. The discouragement is based on the child's *belief* that he or she doesn't belong (whether or not it is true); the misbehavior is the child's "mistaken" way of seeking belonging and significance. The mistake happens when a child believes, "I don't belong, so I'll find belonging by hitting my brother when he tries to grab my cookie." *Big* mistake! As you may recall from Chapter 6, the truth of a situation is often less important than a child's perceptions about that situation. It does not matter that the child *does* belong and family members *do believe* the child is a significant and important person. Behavior is shaped by what the child herself believes about her place in the world—which can change from moment to moment. Each of us is motivated to action by the core beliefs we form from our own inner thoughts, perceptions, and feelings, as well as by the words and actions of significant people in our lives.

It is important to remember that misbehaving children are not consciously aware of their need for belonging or their mistaken beliefs about how to achieve it. It is not important that they be aware. It *is* important that parents recognize that there is a belief behind every behavior, that their own feelings give them clues to understanding what those beliefs might be, and that they will be more effective in changing behavior when they consider the beliefs in their child's heart. With prayer, patience, and some new ideas, it is possible for parents (and for their children) to choose responsible, appropriate behavior over misguided behavior

The Need for Positive Discipline Teaching Tools

Doesn't it make sense that if a misbehaving child is a discouraged child, one way to end the discouragement is by creating an environment where she can change her belief and know that she belongs? Understanding the link between thoughts, feelings, and behavior frees parents to focus on true discipline, teaching, and encouragement, while discarding punishment (lecturing, humiliating, yelling, or hitting) and reward as two outdated tools that rarely change behavior in the long run. (This fact is actually supported by a great deal of research.)

Discipline that is both *kind* and *firm* at the same time enables parents to be their child's best teacher and encourager. True discipline teaches the lifelong skills of self-discipline, responsibility, cooperation, and problem solving. "Train a child in the way he should go, and when he is old he will not turn from it" (Proverbs 22:6) makes perfect sense when we understand that core beliefs motivate behavior. When we help children change their core beliefs (or develop healthy ones in the first place), they won't depart from the behavior that is motivated by those beliefs.

Looking beyond behavior to the belief *behind* the behavior helps us break through the "misbehavior code" so that we can choose tools of instruction and teaching rather than tools for blind obedience. It is through the long-term parent-child relationship that children learn the value of cooperating and contributing to the family. Furthermore, it is the parent's long-term relationship with the Lord that teaches through example how to love and how to set limits that result in a personal life of self-discipline.

> *...like thirsty plants, children need encouragement; receiving it prevents the drought of discouragement—and the misbehavior that so often follows.*

Without God's grace and a parenting toolbox full of effective tools, dealing with children's misbehavior can be a discouraging process—for parents and for children. "Fathers *(and mothers)*, provoke not your children to anger, lest they be discouraged." (Colossians 3:21, NKJV, emphasis added) Both God's Word and the Mistaken Goal Chart provide a window through which parents can view children with understanding eyes as they unconsciously act out their own discouragement. You and your children can develop mutual respect, dignity, and confidence when you are able to focus on the beliefs behind the misbehavior, rather than only the misbehavior itself.

On the other hand, when parents aren't aware of the concept of belonging and significance and its impact on a child's behavior, a cycle of discouragement begins. Children continue to misbehave, escalating their anger and other negative emotions, while well-meaning parents continue to scold or punish children in an effort to control them from the outside instead of working to create a firm foundation of inner discipline within the child. This robs families of the joy and peace that God desires for His people.

Awareness of the concept that human behavior is based on our sense of belonging and significance and our perception of the world around us, and the discouragement that results when we *don't* have that feeling, is the first big step toward increasing your effectiveness as a parent. After reading this chapter, you will have taken that first step. But there is more that you can do. A significant change in attitude can help you catapult your family toward a more cooperative climate at home: You can choose to change your *own* behavior when children misbehave, rather than attempting to change your children's behavior. Like it or not, parents have the responsibility to change first; children's behavior almost always changes in response. As God has instructed us, "Fathers, do not exasperate your children; instead, bring them up in the training and instruction of the Lord." (Ephesians 6:4)

Mistaken Goal Chart

Jane Nelsen, www.positivediscipline.com

1	2	3	4	5	6	7
The Child's Goal	If the parent/ teacher feels	And tends to react by	And if the child's response is	The belief behind the child's behavior	**Coded messages**	Parent/teacher proactive and empowering responses include
Undue Attention (to keep others busy or to get special service)	Annoyed Irritated Worried Guilty	Reminding Coaxing Doing things for the child he/she could do for him/herself	Stops temporarily but later resumes the same or another disturbing behavior	I count (belong) only when I'm being noticed or getting special service. I'm only important when I'm keeping you busy with me.	**Notice Me** **Involve Me Usefully**	Redirect by involving child in a useful task to gain useful attention; ignore (touch without words); say what you will do, "I love you and ____." (Example: I care about you and will spend time with you later.") Avoid special service; have faith in child to deal with feelings (don't fix or rescue); plan special time; set up routines; engage child in problem-solving; use family/ class meetings; set up nonverbal signals.

Misguided Power (to be boss)	Challenged Threatened Defeated	Fighting or Giving in Thinking "You can't get away with it" or "I'll make you" Wanting to be right	Intensifies behavior. Defiant compliance. Feels he/ she's won when parent/ teacher is upset. Passive Power	I belong only when I'm boss, in control, or proving no one can boss me. You can't make me.	**Let Me Help** **Give Me Choices**	Redirect to positive power by asking for help; offer limited choices; don't fight and don't give in; withdraw from conflict; be firm and kind; act, don't talk; decide what you will do; let routines be the boss; leave and calm down; develop mutual respect; set a few reasonable limits; practice follow-through; use family/class meetings.
Revenge (to get even)	Hurt Disappointed Disbelieving Disgusted	Retaliating Getting even Thinking "How could you do this to me?"	Retaliates Intensifies Escalates the same behavior or chooses another weapon	I don't think I belong so I'll hurt others as I feel hurt. I can't be liked or loved.	**I'm Hurting** **Validate My Feelings**	Acknowledge hurt feelings; avoid feeling hurt; avoid punishment and retaliation; build trust; use reflective listening; share your feelings; make amends; show you care; act, don't talk; encourage strengths; put kids in same boat; use family/ class meetings.
Assumed Inadequacy (to give up and be left alone)	Despair Hopeless Helpless Inadequate	Giving up Doing for Over-helping	Retreats further. Passive No improvement No response	I can't belong since I'm not perfect, so I'll convince others not to expect anything of me; I am helpless & unable; it's no use trying since I won't do it right.	**Don't Give Up On Me** **Show Me A Small Step**	Break task down to small steps; stop all criticism; encourage any positive attempt; have faith in child's abilities; focus on assets; don't pity; don't give up; set up opportunities for success; teach skills/ show how, but don't do for; enjoy the child; build on child's interests; use family/class meetings.

Breaking the Code: How to Use the Mistaken Goal Chart

If you can learn to read the code behind children's behavior in different situations, you can deal effectively with their beliefs instead of just the behavior itself. There are three specific clues that will help you break the code to identify the message behind the misbehavior. Let's examine how parents can understand the message behind a child's misbehavior—and decide what to do about it.

Clue 1: Your Own Feelings in Response to the Behavior

Take a look at Column 2 of the Mistaken Goal Chart in this chapter. Believe it or not, the most powerful tools you have in understanding your child's mistaken goal are your own feelings. For example, Megan's mother felt irritated and annoyed when her daughter whined to go home, a clue that the mistaken goal of Megan's behavior was undue attention. (It is important to realize that the same behavior can happen for different reasons. If Megan's parents had felt challenged or provoked by her behavior, her mistaken goal would have been misguided power, and they might have chosen a different response.) By matching your own feelings when your child misbehaves to the feelings listed in the chart's column 2, you will be able to identify your child's mistaken goal.

Clue 2: Your Usual (Ineffective) Attempts to Stop the Behavior

Do you ever get that "déjà vu" feeling when dealing with your child's behavior? Often parents and children find themselves reliving the same frustrating moments together: the child misbehaves, the parent reacts, the child reacts to the parent, and on and on it goes, like a dance in which everyone knows the steps and just can't stop dancing.

Column 3 of the Mistaken Goal Chart lists ways that parents frequently react to a child's misbehavior. If you see yourself here, be reassured: all parents have these moments. There is one more clue that will help you determine the mistaken goal of your child's behavior.

Clue 3: Your Child's Response to Your Ineffective Action

Megan's mom responded to having her skirt pulled by coaxing and then ignoring Megan, an ineffective response in this situation. Megan retaliated by choosing another tactic, pushing her mother and demanding to go home. The ways that children typically respond to parents' ineffective actions are listed in Column 4 of the chart, and provide another clue to the mistaken goal.

Column 5 tells you the belief behind your child's misbehavior—an important part of responding in an effective way—while Column 6 tells you the plea of your child's heart, the message she is trying to communicate to you. The final column (Column 7) provides suggestions and tools for effectively dealing with both the misbehavior and the belief behind it. (More about *Positive Discipline Tools* in Chapter 8.)

Many parents and teachers make copies of this chart and place it on their desks or refrigerators as a constant reminder to seek understanding of the "belief behind the behavior." And then, right at eye level, is a list of some useful tools to encourage children to form more useful beliefs—and to improve their behavior in the process. As you explore the Mistaken Goals, let the words of Galatians 5:22-23a fill your heart: "But the fruit of the Spirit is love, joy, peace, patience, kindness, goodness, faithfulness, gentleness and self-control." Raising children, no matter how much you love them, is one of life's greatest challenges. The best parenting tools are those that demonstrate the fruit of God's Spirit, no easy task when confronted with a misbehaving child. When parents are willing to change first and choose to act with love, kindness, goodness, gentleness and self-control, they will always be more effective.

Let's take a look at what the Mistaken Goals look like in the real world.

Undue Attention

In many loving homes, children are the center of the family universe. Their needs and feelings always come first (often at the expense of adult needs and feelings), entertainment and educational opportunities are offered on a regular basis, and a huge portion of the family's financial resources are devoted to the children. Many parents are astonished and appalled to discover that much of their children's misbehavior is focused on getting attention.

"Wait a minute," these parents say. "We take our commitment to our children seriously. We give our kids lots of attention; we play with them and read to them and pray for them and buy them the things they want. How could they possibly need *more* attention?" Actually, giving children excessive amounts of attention (even in the name of love) may be part of the problem. Remember, children are always making decisions about how to find belonging and about what "works" in life. If a child decides he belongs only when he is receiving the undivided attention of the adults around him, any interruption in that attention will pose a problem for the child—and eventually, for his parents! (And yes, even negative attention is preferable to children than no attention at all.)

Children are "a heritage from the Lord" (Psalm 127:3) and deserve their parents' attention. But they need to receive attention in ways that encourage them to develop character, cooperation, and respect for the needs and feelings of others. There's a simple rule about manipulation. It goes, "If you think you are being manipulated by your child—you are." When your child behaves in ways that cause you to feel annoyed, irritated, worried, or guilty, he is probably seeking undue attention and special service from you and truly needs to be noticed and involved.

> *Giving children excessive amounts of attention (even in the name of love) may be part of the problem.*

The last column of the Mistaken Goal Chart will give you tools and suggestions for more effective ways to respond. (We will explore these tools in detail in the chapters ahead.) For now, recognizing the belief behind your child's behavior will help you respond kindly and firmly to direct your child in a more positive direction.

Misguided Power

The Lord in His wisdom gave human beings the gift of free will, a gift some parents question when they are standing toe-to-toe with a defiant youngster! Like it or not, the only person you truly have the ability to control is yourself—and any parent can tell you that *self*-control is tough enough sometimes. How easy it is to recognize that need for power in our opponent rather than admit that we, too, are hungry to influence those around us!

The Bible is full of examples of misguided power that we can use to teach our children. For instance, consider David, who as a grown man sometimes let power go to his head as in the story of David and Bathsheba (2 Samuel 11-12). Share with your children the stories about the Good Samaritan and the thief (Luke 10:25-37), Jacob and Esau (Genesis 27), or the story of the Prodigal Son and his older brother (Luke 15:11-32) to help your children understand the consequences of actions driven by a need for power.

Children do need personal power—to make choices, to influence their own lives, and sometimes to experience the consequences of wrong choices. (If you doubt it, consider this: Do you enjoy feeling helpless or victimized? Neither does your child.) In fact, there are phases in a child's development when a thirst for personal power is a typical part of the process, the preschool years and adolescence being the primary examples. However, children need to learn to use their considerable power for other purposes than resisting adults, arguing, and getting their own way. How parents teach these lessons is one of the greatest challenges in parenting.

> *Children need to learn to use their considerable power for other purposes than resisting adults, arguing, and getting their own way.*

Proverbs 16:32 tells us that "Better a patient man than a warrior, a man who controls his temper than one who takes a city." Controlling one's temper—handling conflict calmly and effectively, accepting the different perceptions and feelings of others, and compromising rather than insisting on one's own way—are skills many adults still need to learn. It should come as no surprise that children haven't mastered them yet, either. It may help you see your angry three-year-old (or thirteen-year-old) in a different light if you see her behavior as a plea to "let me help; give me choices." It is both more respectful and more effective to invite a child's cooperation ("Can you help me for a moment?") than to demand her compliance. ("Get over here and do it right now!")

The goal chart and future chapters will provide specific suggestions and tools on coping with misguided power. For now, allow yourself to see your child's heart as well as her less-than-appealing behavior.

THE MISTAKEN GOALS OF MISBEHAVIOR

- Undue Attention

- Misguided Power

- Revenge

- Assumed Inadequacy

Revenge

The Lord may claim vengeance as his own, but that hasn't stopped generations of His people from wanting a little for themselves. Children sometimes feel hurt, misunderstood, or even unloved, and may unconsciously seek to retaliate and feel better for a moment by hurting someone else, either physically or emotionally. Often, that someone is a parent.

Martin was six years old when his father left his mother. In the aftermath, Martin struggled with his anger at his beloved father and mother, his sense of utter powerlessness to repair his family, and his deep sorrow, none of which he could express adequately in words. One afternoon his mother asked him to put away his toys, and Martin exploded. "Dad wouldn't have left if you hadn't been such a crummy wife," he said angrily, with tears streaming down his face. His mother, wounded and shocked, watched wordlessly as Martin ran down the hall to his room and slammed the door.

Was Martin's behavior acceptable? Of course not. But his sense of belonging and significance in his world had been damaged by the changes his family had experienced. Martin returned a few minutes later, said "I'm so sorry, Mom," and sobbed in his mother's arms. Martin's words were ugly, but his mother was able to recognize that they were a plea for understanding and help in dealing with his own hurt. She avoided retaliation herself, and instead focused on helping her son understand his feelings and on coping with the changes the family was facing.

When children act out of a mistaken goal of revenge, parents need to hear the plea behind their behavior, a plea which might have come directly from the words of Scripture: "Turn to me, and have mercy upon me, for I am desolate and afflicted." (Psalm 25:16, NKJV) Responding as the Lord does—with compassion, guidance, hope, and comfort—can help children choose different behavior. Again, we will explore specific tools for helping our hurting children in the chapters ahead.

Assumed Inadequacy

Few things are more worrisome and frustrating for parents than the child who "can't," who won't try new things, or who gives up in a cloud of discouragement at the first sign of disappointment. These are the children who "can't" ride a bicycle, who "can't" do math, and who will never try out for an athletic team or the school orchestra. Parents often respond by coaxing, doing too much for the child, or giving up in despair themselves. ("I guess you're right; maybe you can't ride a bike.")

Children who act out of the mistaken goal of assumed inadequacy believe they can't belong and are, more than anything else, deeply discouraged about their own worth and abilities. What they need from parents is faith—something than can be difficult to hold onto when it seems a child won't even try. But remember, "Faith is being sure of what we hope for and certain of what we do not see." (Hebrews 11:1) Deeply discouraged children rely on their parents not to give up, to show faith daily, and to help them find small steps so they can begin to experience success and confidence. If the Lord never gives up on us, who are we to give up on our children?

The Mistaken Goal Chart in Action

The Mistaken Goal Chart can take time to understand; it is, after all, a different approach to misbehavior than most parents have experienced before, and it requires willingness to see family life in a different way. The results, however, can be well worth the effort. One of the authors recalls a parent who learned about the mistaken goals in a parenting class several years ago. As she tried to digest the power of the goal chart, Margo began to think out loud, "If I always do what I've always done, then I'll always get what I've always gotten. That's just plain dumb! Since I understand misbehavior differently now, I'll do something differently now. It might result in my child making different choices, too … and I like that!"

Let's take one more look at how a child might express one of the mistaken goals. One of the authors, Mary Hughes, tells the story of her oldest daughter's response to having twin babies arrive in the home. In this story we see the three clues at work with a case of classic misbehavior.

When Eric and Wendy were born nearly 40 years ago, Erin was barely 4 years old. One week before the birth-date, Mom and Dad learned they would be having twins, so they didn't have much time to let Erin know that she would be the big sister of *two* babies.

Erin laughed when Mom and Dad told her they would be bringing two babies home from the hospital "You can't have two babies, Mommy! That's funny!" she exclaimed. Mom and Dad were both very excited and rather nervous. No one in either family had any experience in raising twins; nor did anyone they knew have any experience to share on the topic.

Erin's reaction to two real babies was a resolute request to "… take the boy back, Mommy; he's too noisy and too big. We can keep the girl-baby. She's so pretty and little." Even though her parents laughed then, and still do, Erin was very serious in her request. She could handle *one* baby just fine, but *two*? No way—that meant Mommy and Daddy would each have one, and then who would pay attention to Erin?

Erin often wedged herself between the two babies when they'd be on a blanket on the floor so she could have Wendy to herself.

Mary continues to share, "I felt irritated and annoyed by Erin's behavior, and I usually reacted by sending her to her room 'until she could play nicely with her brother *and* her sister.' Erin always found ways to let me know she resented having to share her parents' undivided attention with the twins. Even though the three of them are best friends as adults, I can easily recall the many ways Erin reminded me in those early years, through her behavior, how rudely I ousted her from the center of our parental universe."

The Belief Behind the Behavior

Undoubtedly there are parents who will empathize with Mary as they read her story. Erin, as do many other first-born children, felt pushed aside, no longer the only apple of her parents' eyes. What Erin didn't know was that parents have huge hearts that make room for each child, and that a parent's love is ever-deepening and can encircle all their children.

At the time her children were born, Mary had not yet encountered Positive Discipline and did not understand the mistaken goal behind Erin's behavior. If she had, she might have been able to respond differently. Let's replay the scene as it might happen today:

"Come here for a moment, Erin," Mary called to her daughter. "The babies are asleep and your Dad and I would like to tell you a story."

Erin walked dejectedly over and flopped down next to her parents; it had been a long day, and she had spent a good deal of it alone in her room. Mary pulled the coffee table closer, and Erin noticed with curiosity that on it were several candles.

Mary picked up a tall blue candle and lit it with a match. "See this candle?" she asked. "This candle is me, and the flame is my love. When I met your daddy, I gave him all my love." Mary picked up a big yellow candle and lit it with her blue one. "Then, a few years later, God sent us a beautiful baby girl named Erin…"

"That's me!" Erin crowed delightedly. "Is that candle mine? I love purple!"

"Yes," Mary smiled, "and when you were born, we gave you all our love." Mary lit the purple candle with her own and set it next to the others in a holder. "Now your daddy has all my love, and you have all my love, and I still have all my love left."

Erin watched the candles dance, fascinated by the flickering flames.

"Guess what happened next?" Mary went on. "God knew how much we loved you, so He sent us two more babies, Wendy and Eric." And Mary picked up two birthday candles, one pink and one blue, and lit them. "Now Daddy has all my love, and you have all my love, and the twins have all my love, and I still have all my love left. Because that's the way love is—no matter how much you give away, you still have lots left to share. See how much bright love there is in our family?"

Erin was silent for a moment, and then she asked, "Can I light the twins' candles with mine? I want to share my love."

If Mary had known then what she knows now, Erin might have been able to learn much earlier and more easily that she didn't need to misbehave to earn a share of her parents' love and attention.

Understanding the mistaken goals of misbehavior will not eliminate misbehavior from your family. There will still be moments of frustration, anger, and regret, for all of you. But understanding the mistaken goals can help you be your best as a parent, to respond from the fruits of the Spirit, and to help your children become the Godly, capable, confident young adults they were meant to be.

Chapter 8

Positive Discipline Tools:
What's in Your Parenting Tool Kit?

Betty and Jim started up the hill for their nightly walk. "Honey, I'm so discouraged," Betty said with a sigh. "I can't seem to stop yelling and nagging at John. He used to listen to me whether I yelled or not. Now, he just hangs his head down and says, 'There you go again, Mom. I hate it when you yell at me.' He's only 8, but I get so exasperated when he says that! I start yelling all over again. And I don't follow through on the things I say to him. I don't know what to do or say when he won't help with the chores, and he picks on his sister all the time. I've tried taking away his television privileges, and last week I told him he couldn't go on the youth group campout because he hadn't cleaned his room. But it doesn't seem like anything is changing. I'm tired of being 'mean old Mom' but I don't know how to stop."

Jim put a reassuring arm around his wife's shoulders. "I know what you mean, Betty. It seems like we used to be able to just ask John for help, and maybe remind him a time or two, but he isn't listening anymore. When I raise my voice he says, 'You sound like my gym teacher. Can't you just talk to me in a normal voice?' We don't have much control over him," Jim chuckled ruefully. "For that matter, we don't seem to have much control over ourselves, either. I talked with George Barnes at church yesterday. He said he rarely yells at Anthony—they have family meetings at their house to figure out the chores, the calendar, and even plan some family fun times. Maybe we just need to learn a little more about our job as parents. Why don't we go to that parenting class that started at church two weeks ago? We can't be such bad parents, Betty. I just think we need some new ideas and skills."

Information and ideas are good things. But even when you are armed with an understanding of your child's developmental ages and stages and a new misbehavior goal chart to help you understand your child's mistaken beliefs, you still must deal with the misbehavior itself. Like many parents, Betty and Jim had realized that punishment, nagging, and yelling are not effective ways to guide children's behavior. But a very important question remains: what should parents do? Society tells parents that misbehaving children need to 'pay' for their misbehavior.

Well-intentioned parents often follow these mistaken words of "wisdom," and find themselves blindly pinned somewhere between punishment and rewards with no helpful discipline tool in hand.

We have seen in previous chapters—and in the scene above—that neither punishment nor rewards "work" over the long term to teach children the life skills necessary to thrive as developing Christians and capable young adults. Discipline that swings from extremely firm to excessively kind is not helpful either. Knowing that 'a misbehaving child is discouraged' takes a radical shift in thinking. Parents must move from an attitude of "How can I *get* that kid to …?" to "How can I help that kid to *know I care*? And how can I encourage that kid to make better choices about her behavior?"

Parents need tools of encouragement "to help a child do better," rather than tools of discouragement to make a child "stop doing that." Tools that encourage *give heart to* the child. (*Coeur* is the French word for heart, and is the root word of encouragement.) Tools that discourage *rip the heart right out of* the child. Listen to the words of Jeremiah on behalf of believers who had strayed from the path of righteousness: "Correct me, Lord, but only with justice—not in your anger, lest you reduce me to nothing." (Jeremiah 10:24) True discipline engages the heart rather than breaking the spirit. True discipline is justice and compassion at work. If God our Father can extend his grace to us even when we sin, how much more should we extend grace to our children? Do we raise them with the "letter of the law"—with punishment and shame—or with grace that offers belonging, encouragement, *and* guidance in making good choices in life? As Paul told the Romans, "You are not under the law, but under grace." (Romans 6:14)

> True discipline engages the heart rather than breaking the spirit.

Positive Discipline tools grow respectful relationships between parents and children, keep children accountable for their behavior without relying on punishment or rewards, and keep families in balance on the continuum of kind *and* firm without swinging radically from one extreme to the other. Positive Discipline tools and God's Word will help you:

- grow faithful young people
- increase the internalization of scriptural truths
- build respectful relationships among family members
- teach skills to help children thrive, rather than merely survive
- encourage parents and children to learn from mistakes
- help parents maintain authority without being authoritarian

Before looking at the Positive Discipline tools, this chapter will explore three tools specific for Christian homes. Then we will look at six Positive Discipline tools to help you experience success no matter what your child's mistaken goal might be. The remainder of the chapter will focus on proactive tools parents can use for each of the four mistaken goals—tools that will help you get beyond yelling and punishment to respect, cooperation, and increased family harmony.

Three Discipline Tools Especially for Christian Homes

Three Christian practices are especially effective tools for Christian parents: these are Scripture, prayer, and opportunities for faith development. Richard J. Foster in his landmark book, *Celebration of Discipline: The Path to Spiritual Growth*, 20th Anniversary Edition, Harper, 1978, p. 6, explains how living a spiritually disciplined life can keep us connected to the Holy Spirit who would empower us with the strength to parent as we desire. Foster speaks of discipline as a liberating and transforming choice in his first chapter. He summarizes his reasoning for leading a spiritually disciplined life as a parent by saying "God has ordained the disciplines of the spiritual life as the means by which we are placed where He can bless us."

When parents live a spiritually-disciplined life, their homes are blessed, and God's grace is at work in each member of the family. Scripture, prayer, and opportunities for faith development strengthen a home and enable parents to practice both their faith and Positive Discipline principles.

Scripture

Scripture is God's voice teaching through stories and metaphors about everyday living. Using the Bible as a living letter from God is a Christian parent's privilege. Rather than using Scripture to condemn and shame us, God intends for parents and children alike to gain wisdom, comfort, hope and strength from Scripture.

The Old Testament contains numerous stories of the courageous actions of godly men and women—and even a child or two! Take the story of David and Goliath. In churches all over the world, this story is used most often to show how faithful people can do great things when relying on God's strength and power. Rarely is much made of the fact that David is just a boy. In fact, King Saul rebukes David's enthusiasm to fight Goliath when he says: "You are not able to go out against this Philistine and fight him; *you are only a boy*, and he (Goliath) has been a fighting man from his youth." (1 Samuel 17:33)

This is a story of trust and faith on the part of a small boy who, despite all worldly odds, had an intimate knowledge of God and His ways. It is a very reassuring story for children for several reasons. It illustrates that reliance on God dwarfs the significance of worldly or physical stature. It contains wisdom for parents who seek God's strength and wisdom when facing the numerous Goliaths in today's world.

God equips a child to face the giant in his life in this story, and to the amazement of many adults, God can use children, even when they disobey, to teach us lessons about what really matters in life. In the story of David and Goliath, David chooses five stones from the stream to put in his pouch. When it came time to slay *his* Goliath, David chose only one small stone, and it destroyed the giant. Tim Kimmel, a Christian parenting teacher, suggests that parents become gatherers of five smooth stones to help them overcome the everyday obstacles to parenting with courage. Kimmel suggests that parents need truth, rest, quiet, prayer, and laughter to be courageous parents.

Now picture yourself in David's shoes, gathering smooth stones from the living water (Jesus). These stones are inscribed with the qualities that you want to grow in your children.

Perhaps your stones say courage, responsibility, reliability, success, faithfulness, trust, love, joy, peace, or hope. Each quality you inscribe on a stone is one you hope to encourage in your child's character. You can find at least one companion Scripture to help you and your child develop that quality. Use these Scriptures, along with your church's instruction, to teach your children. Discover other magnificent stories throughout the Bible. Create an imaginary pouch of stones for each of your children, and fill it to the brim with gifts of scriptural instruction.

Prayer

In the Christian home, prayer can and should become a constant companion. But prayer should be more than the obligatory "Now I lay me down to sleep" or "Bless this food." Prayer is both an important tool for communicating with God and a source of real strength from moment to moment. Prayer can become a cornerstone for your entire family.

> *Prayer is important to your own spiritual growth, and your children will learn from your example.*

Christian homes can be lacking in prayer for reasons each of us can understand. You may have said, "After all, the kids are too young to understand how to pray." Or maybe you said, "We can teach them about prayer when they learn to read the Bible." Or could you have said, "They'll learn how to pray in Sunday School." You might even have said, "There just isn't time to pray—we're just too busy keeping everything going." Children often have as many activities as their parents do, and the hectic pace seems to quicken as they grow. Some parents even fear that their children will think family prayer isn't "cool."

Someone once said, "A day without prayer is a day without "Son-shine." Throughout the stages of parenting, prayer is an integral part in surviving the daily crises of life with children. Ecclesiastes 3:1 tells us "There is a time for everything, and a season for every activity under heaven." Prayer is essential for listening to God and for asking God for the help we so desperately need as parents. Prayer is important to your own spiritual growth, and your children will learn from your example. Prayer can become a part of every family meeting and a reassuring end to every day. You can keep prayer requests on the family dinner table or on the family meeting agenda board. Let your children learn to lead the family in prayer; honor their spirits without correcting their words. In doing so, you will draw them closer to God.

There are times when parents must use wisdom in praying with children. Several well-known Christian parenting sources encourage parents to pray with children about their behavior—and misbehavior. While this can be a wonderful opportunity to learn and grow, parents must pay careful attention to what their children are learning and deciding. Consider the following:

- **Should I pray with a child before (or after) a spanking?**
  Well, we don't advocate spanking, so we would hope the opportunity never arises. We have, however, spoken with children who wonder, "How can God love me and still want my parents to hurt me?" Remember, discipline is intended to *teach*. The attitudes and actions children need to learn can be communicated much more

effectively by kind, firm action than by corporal punishment, even when the action is preceded by prayer.

- **Should I make my child pray for forgiveness when he misbehaves?**
  Asking forgiveness can be a healing act that relieves guilt and restores the bonds of trust and love. However, it can help a child accept responsibility for his actions and encourage him to try again when parents (and by example, God the Father) also recognize a child's strengths and right choices. For instance, a parent might pray with a child, "Father, I thank you for Robby's honesty in admitting that he stole a dollar from my wallet. Help us both to make better choices, to listen to each other, and to work to always be honest with each other." Remember, a child is as likely to need your forgiveness as well as God's.

- **Should I pray for forgiveness if I lose my temper with my child?**
  By all means—but be sure you learn from your own mistakes, just as you expect your child to. Repentance and forgiveness imply a desire to *change*; if you find your-self praying for forgiveness for the same offense over and over, perhaps it is time to discover why that particular problem keeps occurring and to take steps to prevent it. Like it or not, change begins first with parents. Parents must also be as willing to forgive their children as God is to forgive them. "Bear with each other and forgive whatever grievances you may have against one another. Forgive as the Lord forgave you." (Colossians 3:13)

- **Should I quote Scripture to make my child "shape up?"**
  As with so many things in life, attitude is everything. If you use Scripture as a weapon to bludgeon your child or to heap on blame and shame, you are unlikely to motivate behavior change in ways other than revenge, discouragement, and disil-lusionment with God. Quoting (or memorizing) Scripture and praying together as parent and child to build up a child's courage and understanding is helpful; the misuse of Scripture to bathe a misbehaving child in guilt is not.

- **Should I expect my child to obey me the first time I correct her?**
  Each of us—adult and child—has a responsibility to learn from mistakes and wrong choices. But few of us can promise that we will *never* make the same mistake again. Repetition and patience are an essential part of effective parenting, especially when your children are young. Expecting instant obedience and "one-time only" behavior is unrealistic, even for a cooperative and responsible child, and will only frustrate both of you. It is probably wisest to pray for patience for *yourself*, rather than praying for obedience from your child.

Opportunities for Faith Development

No matter the age, children raised in Christian homes need opportunities to develop a personal, active, vital faith. In James 2:17 we are given the explanation of the relationship between faith and works: "In the same way, faith by itself, if it is not accompanied by action, is dead."

Chelsea, five years old, noticed the moving van next door and ran to her Mom. "I want to bake some cookies for the new people, okay Mommy?" Chelsea said. "You can help me." Chelsea knew that her family's church shares cookies with visitors. In this way, newcomers are given the opportunity for fellowship and members—even little ones—are given the opportunity to serve. This is how real faith develops, as well as a feeling of self-worth and a strong desire to contribute to others, the quality Alfred Adler called "social interest."

When parents take advantage of these everyday opportunities to teach their children, they are cultivating a sense of belonging and connectedness that can actually prevent misbehavior. Sometimes adults aren't aware that it is in the little, mundane moments of the day that children are watching what is done and said. Day in and day out this observation takes place; yet it still surprises us that our own "actions speak louder than words." Chelsea witnessed her Mom's giving spirit and it encouraged her to be a "giver" and a "welcoming person" like Mommy.

Other avenues abound for Christian parents who are looking for ways to connect their children to faith-developing learning opportunities. Maybe you have read about children who saw homeless children sleeping on cold concrete on the evening television news and actually talked their parents into taking them (and their own pillows and blankets) down to warm the homeless children. These children couldn't have ministered to others without parents who cared enough to listen to their children's voices of faith.

There are some key benefits for families of faith who regularly attend church together. Children can become involved with significant adults (other than their own parents) who offer possibilities for teaching, role modeling, and mentoring children. This can be very important as children grow into the teen years. In fact, as we have already learned, recent research indicates that teenagers who regularly attend church tend to have a greater sense of self-esteem and are at less risk for harmful behaviors than teens who do not attend. Having adults outside their own family whom they (and you) trust helps your children through the sometimes-difficult transition to adulthood. Becoming an active part of a church community soon after moving to a new area also helps families consciously re-form a faithful circle of support. The Search

Institute, out of Minneapolis, Minnesota, lists being part of a religious community for one or more hours per week as one of forty assets needed for healthy youth. (Visit www.search-institute.org for more on-line information about the Search Institute's 40 Developmental Assets).

One of Positive Discipline's strengths is its focus on preventing misbehavior by creating opportunities for connection, contribution, and cooperation. When parents provide real life opportunities during the years that their child's faith is developing, they build a powerful protective hedge against misbehavior and a powerful incentive to live out their Christian faith in love and service to others.

Six Positive Discipline Tools

There are six Positive Discipline tools we will explore in this part of our chapter for a parent to include in his or her toolbox; tools that will help create belonging, a sense of connection, and the development of personal responsibility. (For additional tools see: *Positive Discipline Parenting Tools: 52 Cards to Improve Your Parenting Skills*, Jane Nelsen and Adrian Garsia; order from www.empoweringpeople.com)

They are:

> *When parents provide real life opportunities during the years that their child's faith is developing, they build a powerful protective hedge against misbehavior and a powerful incentive to live out their Christian faith in love and service to others.*

1. curiosity questions
2. limited choices
3. consequences vs. solutions
4. routines
5. positive time-out
6. follow-through

Curiosity Questions

Do you sometimes find it difficult to avoid the temptation to lecture or moralize when your children misbehave? Can you truly *listen* to your child's explanations? Do you recognize this common verbal household duel?

PARENT: "Why did you *do* that?"
CHILD: "I don't know!"

Parents sometimes *tell* children what they think, feel, and should do instead of *asking* them what they think, feel, or should do. One approach creates resistance and defensiveness; the other invites children to become aware of their own internal processes and to participate in finding solutions, the beginning of good judgment and wisdom. Even Jesus didn't go around "telling" others what to do. He taught in parables, inviting his listeners to draw their own conclusions. (Matthew 13:13)

Curiosity questions are those parents ask when they don't already know the answer and when they are genuinely interested in listening (and children always know the difference). They are not asked to humiliate, shame, or discourage the wrongdoer. Curiosity questions are asked in order to learn by examining the situation together. They give clues to what a person can do differently next time.

Jesus frequently modeled the use of curiosity questions for us. Take this story in Luke 10:25-28 (emphasis added), for example:

On one occasion an expert in the law stood up to test Jesus. "Teacher," he asked, "what must I do to inherit eternal life?" "*What* is written in the Law?" He replied. "*How* do you read it?" The man answered: "'Love the Lord your God with all your heart and with all your soul and with all your strength and with all your mind;'" and, 'Love your neighbor as yourself.'" "You have answered correctly," Jesus replied. "Do this and you will live."

What, who, where, when, and *how* are curiosity questions. You may notice that *why* isn't on the list. We do have a reason: *Why* often puts a person on the defensive and can sound more like an interrogation than curiosity, unless it is asked with genuine interest, such as, "*Why* did you think that would be a good choice?"

Additional curiosity questions sound like this: "*What* happened? How do you feel about this? *What* could you do differently next time? *How* can I help? *When* did you first realize you had made a mistake?" Each of these questions is open-ended and designed to help children decide what they should do.

After all, who knows the most about the situation? Unless you are a skilled mind reader, your child is the expert on his own feelings and behavior. Try picturing the last time you asked your child, "Why did you *do* that?" Curiosity questions become your "spyglass," your way of gazing into your child's mind, soul, and heart. Next time you think "why," remember that together you and your child can create a valuable learning situation out of any mistake or misbehavior by using curiosity questions.

Mistakes are sometimes viewed as "sins," but more often they are valuable learning opportunities when curiosity questions are used. Jane Nelsen answered a question from a third-grade teacher that provides a wonderful example. The teacher wasn't sure that "flipping a card" would help a student make a better choice the next time (the consequence in her school's discipline system for misbehavior is to flip a card, a type of punishment that dictates the penalty he will pay). The teacher began by saying, "I'm wondering if what I'm attempting with the help of third graders will work. I had another student call someone a name in front of me today, as a test. Instead of having him flip a card, I asked him about his behavior, some acceptable solutions for the next time, and sent him on his way. This so goes against how I have always done things that I'm afraid to let go, although I fully realize that flipping cards wasn't working…"

Jane replied, "You need to give yourself a big pat on the back for being open enough to see more respectful possibilities. From your own wisdom you used the Positive Discipline tool we call "curiosity questions." You helped him explore his behavior (instead of lecturing him about it), and then asked him to use his own thinking and problem-solving skills to find some solutions (instead of telling him what to do). It only makes sense that this would be more effective because you have involved him in the process and treated him with dignity and respect. What great motivators!"

Curiosity questions are just one way of giving children choices to help them use their thinking skills and to give them power in acceptable ways.

Limited Choices

God has blessed us with free will—the ability to make choices. The Bible describes well the relationship that God wants to have with us, one where we *choose* Him. And let's face it every human being alive wants choices. Parents sometimes get into the habit of "telling or demanding," and then "resorting to commanding." Parents intend their threats and bribes to motivate children, but it rarely works for long: "If you don't get dressed now, young man, you'll be late for football practice—again!" (Threat) "C'mon, Mandy. Pick up your toys right now. I'll stop for an ice-cream cone on the way to dance lessons if you get them all picked up in 10 minutes." (Bribe)

Anything that begins with "if" has a corresponding "then" phrase on its heels. A more effective approach begins with "when" or "as soon as" and follows with "then"; it takes a directive out of the threat-bribe continuum. "*When* you put away your school things, *then* we can leave for football practice." "*As soon as* you put away your school things, *then* we can leave for football practice." The child can choose not to put away his school things, and in so doing is also choosing not to go to football practice. Either choice must be okay with you for this to be effective. In other words, don't imply that children have a choice if you don't intend to offer one. We live in an age of information. Sorting through it all takes great skill and discernment. Either we learn this skill or perish in the sea named Choices. Allowing children to make choices grants them an appropriate sense of personal power and prevents them from insisting (often by way of tantrums), "You're not the boss of me!" For instance, even young children can choose what to wear when given a choice between two items.

Be sure that the choices you offer your child are all choices you can live with. "Do you want to go to bed now?" is *not* the choice. You could ask, "Do you want to go to bed now or in five minutes? You decide." There is something very powerful about adding, "You decide." How would you feel if you were the child?

If there is no choice about bedtime you can say, "Its bedtime," and you can kindly and firmly lead your child to his room. But the child *could* choose his pajamas, whether to brush his teeth before or after the story, what stuffed animal he will take to bed, and whether to have the light on or off.

An "either-or" statement may not be a real choice. It *isn't* a choice when you say "either come in for dinner now or you will go to time-out." A child should be given at least two positive things to choose from. Only give a child a choice such as, "You can choose to clean your toys up now or after dinner," when either option is acceptable to you. Otherwise say something like, "You can choose to put your blocks or your cars away first. Which will you choose?"

Smart parents begin offering choices early in the child-raising years. This gives children the opportunity to practice in situations without dire consequences for making wrong decisions. The ability to make wise decisions on the big issues parents dread ("Should I have sex with my boyfriend?" "Everyone else is having a beer—should I?") is built throughout a child's lifetime; it isn't a quality that magically springs up at the age of sixteen. Start choice-making opportunities today if your goal is to grow adults who will make sound decisions tomorrow.

Routines

Bedtimes, meals, homework, chores—each of these words bring to mind the need for routines. From the time we get up in the morning to the time we go to bed, human beings are creatures of habit—and habit is the result of good (or bad) routines. Young children, especially, thrive on routines—and they are at their creative best in helping parents design meaningful routines. Routines need not be set in stone; rather, routines need to be flexible, as well as firm, to be helpful.

Mark, age six, tried to tell his new babysitter how he brushed his teeth *before* (rather than after) he put on his clothes in the morning. The new babysitter, Belinda, just replied, "I don't really see what difference it makes. Get your shirt on first; then we'll go in and brush your teeth." Mark started to cry and said, "I don't like you; you're mean. You're not doing it right! I'm gonna tell my Mommy on you!"

> Start choice-making opportunities today if your goal is to grow adults who will make sound decisions tomorrow.

Mark's mom was wiser than both Mark and Belinda. When Mark told his mom about how "mean" the new babysitter was, Mom asked Mark, "Tell me what happened, Mark." After hearing how the babysitter didn't "let him get his teeth brushed first" before getting dressed, Mark's Mom suggested making a picture chart of their daily routine, so that when Belinda came to baby-sit again she would know what to do. Mark agreed that was a great idea—then she'd "do it right." Mark didn't care about what time things happened, but he *did* care about the order in which things happened.

Preschoolers can help create routines rather than having adults dictate what *should* happen and when. As children get older, they are quite capable of establishing their own routines from start to finish. Giving children permission to "make a plan" honors the child's need for influence over decisions that directly affect him. When adults *tell* children how the routine will go, it may feel more like a punishment than a teaching or discipline tool.

One way of using routines is to create a routine chart with your child. (You can have a chart for mornings, one for bedtime, and perhaps another for homework or chore-time on Saturday. Note that this is not a sticker or reward chart; it is simply a "map" of your child's routine.) Invite your child to help you list on a large poster board the steps in his routine. If you are working on a bedtime routine, you and your child might decide to brush his teeth and wash his face, put on pajamas, read two stories, say a prayer, and have a good night hug.

You can illustrate your chart with pictures clipped from magazines or, better yet, with photographs of your child doing these tasks. You can even decorate the chart with glitter and stars. Then, if your child gets off track or struggles to cooperate, you can say, "What's next on your bedtime chart?" The routine becomes the boss, and children love to run and check their charts. You might be surprised at just how effective this simple tool is.

Create routines—for getting to school, for doing homework, for getting to bed—that work for your family, then stick with them. Routines can work magic in inviting cooperation from children. (For more on routines in school-related matters such as homework, see *Parenting through the School Years . . . and Beyond!* by Mike Brock, available through www.empoweringpeople.com, www.mikebrock.org, or major online services.)

Consequences and Solutions

Consequences are often helpful for misbehavior that is repetitive—misbehavior that has become a habit. There are two kinds of consequences: natural and logical.

Natural consequences happen as a result of what we do or say. For example, if you don't eat your dinner, you will get hungry. If you make a snowman without mittens, your hands will get cold. Natural consequences work best when parents get out of the way and allow children to learn from their own choices. (Curiosity questions can help: "Boy, your hands look *cold!* Can you think of a way to warm them up?")

Logical consequences are lessons parents or teachers 'think up' that will teach children to make a different choice the next time a similar situation arises. The best consequences are those that children know in advance, and those designed to find a *solution* to the problem, not a thinly disguised punishment or "payback" for misbehavior. (And kids always know the difference.) Jane Nelsen is known for this quote: "No more logical consequences, at least hardly ever!" All too often, adults are proud of the 'consequences' they think up for a misbehavior that they want to 'cure.' In a couple of paragraphs we'll divulge some clues for ensuring that a logical consequence isn't perceived as a punishment. We're NOT saying that it won't be tough for the adult or child involved; but we ARE saying we want the consequence to teach rather than preach or screech! Here's an example of how to focus on solutions:

Ryan is five and loves to wrestle with Mitch, his five-year-old cousin. Much like puppies in a box, they roll and grab—and inevitably, someone gets a finger in his eye or a foot in his groin. Because Ryan's parents recognize that this situation is likely to occur more than once, they decide to sit down at a family meeting with Ryan and Mitch and look for solutions to the wrestling dilemma. They decide together that when the boys want to wrestle, they must first ask an adult to act as referee or they will have to choose a quiet game.

Ryan suggested that the boys take karate classes to learn more about physical safety. And together, everyone came up with "The Plan," which they wrote down and posted on the refrigerator. According to "The Plan," in order to wrestle, both boys have to agree before they begin that *both* of them want to wrestle; when either one says 'uncle' that's the code word to stop wrestling. They brainstormed a list of helpful things to do when someone gets hurt, like get ice, get a tissue, offer a hug, or suggest a quiet activity. And they agreed in advance that there would be no more wrestling that day if someone got hurt, even a little bit.

Mom and Dad had learned at their parenting workshop that it's a good idea to involve the children in helping figure out a solution, and that a good solution needed to meet the following "4 R's and an H" formula to avoid being perceived as punishment:

1st **R** = respectfully given
2nd **R** = related to the misbehavior
3rd **R** = reasonable
4th **R** = revealed in advance of the misbehavior whenever possible and
1 **H** = helpful to everyone involved; not hurtful to anyone involved

The day after the family meeting, both boys gave each other the go-ahead to wrestle; Ryan got pinned to the floor and suffered a rug burn on his elbow. As soon as Ryan yelped, "uncle," Mitch stopped wrestling. Dad reminded him that he had to do something to help Ryan feel better by asking a curiosity question, "What could you do to help?" Mitch ran to the bathroom for a cool cloth, and soon Ryan's rug burn was feeling okay.

The boys forgot about the part of the plan that included no more wrestling that day. Dad simply asked, "What part of your plan are you forgetting right now?" The boys had to stop wrestling while they thought about an answer. It didn't take them long to remember; then they checked the list of choices for what they could do instead of wrestling. They decided to go outside to throw and catch baseballs.

This perfect little scene may not work so perfectly forever, but it will work as long as it is a viable solution for everyone concerned. They can follow their old plan or go back to the drawing board and create a new plan. Often parents think that one consequence or plan or solution should be the final word—that a solution or plan should end all the misbehavior with no future discussion or challenges. More often, a situation like Ryan and Mitch are experiencing will come up again, perhaps even over a similar behavior. Perhaps even more important than the details of The Plan is the fact that Mitch, Ryan, and their parents are learning the skills to resolving difficulties with mutual respect and dignity, skills they can rely on whenever a new problem occurs.

Sometimes it seems like too much work to involve children in solutions, instead of just being a parental dictator who insists that children do what you say and "stop this ruckus once and for all!" Involving the children in creating a plan for handling a troubling situation helps them invest in the solutions they discover and practice their conflict-resolution skills. They can also learn social skills such as negotiation and compromise, as well as contribution and cooperation.

You may have noticed that little difference exists between "consequences that teach" and "solutions." In most situations, a good consequence is the same as a positive solution. Negative consequences (usually designed to "make that kid *pay*") more often resemble punishment. With a little practice, parents using Positive Discipline tools can lead their families toward becoming expert solution-makers.

Positive Time-Out

Parents often use time out as a sort of punishment. "Go to your room and think about what you did!" they tell their children. And then they wonder why children never seem to come to the "correct" conclusions! (And have you ever thought about how silly it is to assume you can control what your child will think about?)

Time out has been used in a number of ways. Some parents count to three, then send a misbehaving child to time out. Some parents set a timer and make a child sit and think in a chair or on the stairs ("one minute for each year of age"). Some parents make their children stand in a corner, press their noses to the wall, or suffer some sort of humiliation or indignity, all in the name of discipline. Other parents spend their child's time-out trying to get that child to *stay* in time out! Time-out is best used as a "positive" time-out—that is, a time for your child to get a grip on his emotions, calm down, and regain the ability to control his behavior. (It is usually true, as well, that parents benefit more from time outs than do their children!)

> Involving the children in creating a plan for handling a troubling situation helps them invest in the solutions they discover and practice their conflict-resolution skills.

As we have said earlier, children do better when they feel better. A positive time-out should be designed to help the child feel better. Some people mistakenly believe this is "rewarding" the misbehavior. That is because they forget the second part of "feel better" which is to "do better." Children really will *do* better when they *feel* better.

A "cool off" time-out is not punitive when it is done the Positive Discipline way. You and your child can build a comfortable time-out spot anywhere in the home, and stock it with items that help your child recognize and regain control of his unruly emotions. This might include plush animals, soft music, books, and a comfortable cushion for sitting. You can let him know that he can rejoin the family when he feels better *and* when he can get along.

Remember Mitch and Ryan? As part of their Plan, they and their parents designed ways for them to cool off and get along. The boys have created several places around the house for some quiet-time when they need it. Mom has learned to say, "I need some quiet for a bit. It's too noisy in here. Do you need my help to find something else to do?" To which the boys now say, "No, Mom—we can go do our Lite Brite™ together or play one of our music tapes or…" They have even discussed how different people need different amounts of quiet-time and like to do different things while taking time away from the family. No one counts how old you are to time a time-out anymore, no one yells, and no one probes anyone after time-out about "what they learned while in time-out."

Actually, time-out has never been the problem. What parents have done in the name of time-out has sometimes created problems. Time-out wasn't originally designed to be a punishment: God suggested long ago that a quiet time with Him be an enjoyable and helpful time, a time to provide focus for the day, a way to re-group, or a time to pray. Jesus himself found time to pull away from the crowds in order to regain strength before coming back to His ministry. (Matthew 14:23) Unfortunately, violence, rage, abuse, aggression, and disrespect occur even in Christian families—as do guilt, shame, and deep regret. While all parents occasionally lose their temper, harming children either by words or deeds can often be avoided when everyone learns to take time to cool off, to seek guidance, and to regain control.

Positive time out, like many Positive Discipline skills, takes patience, the ability to model what you teach, and the courage to keep trying after mistakes. Remember, you can't have a "wrong" feeling (neither can your children), but you can sometimes *act* in hurtful or inappropriate ways. Positive time-out gives everyone time to consider the consequences of their actions, to manage their weaknesses, and to develop awareness of their feelings—and the consequences those feelings can have when out of control. Some families we know take "family time-outs." For example, they take the phone off the hook at supper time, let the answering machine answer the calls before they invade the family meeting, turn off the TV one night each week, make the Blackberry phones (or any other 'smart' device) off-limits for a period of each day, or make Sunday evening a time 'just for the family.' Some parents we know do their best housecleaning/yard-work when releasing pent-up anger; others garden, sew, or do crafts.

What's your version of time-out? What are you teaching your children about time-out? The challenge is yours: you can make time-out in your home an encouraging, empowering experience. We think you'll be glad you did. (For more information, see *Positive Time-Out and Over 50 Ways to Avoid Power Struggles in Homes and Classrooms*, Jane Nelsen, Ed. D., 1999, Prima Publishing.)

Follow-Through

Follow-through is doing whatever you say you'll do. As grandmothers the world over have said, "Say what you mean and mean what you say." Believe it or not, children learn trust when parents follow through; they learn they can rely on mom and dad to do what they've said they would do.

Mitch and Ryan had brainstormed some playing options should they get too rough and need to quit wrestling for the day. The boys cooperated with The Plan, and chose another play activity off their list. What might happen if Mom decided they could have 'one more try' before they had to quit wrestling? One more 'try' wasn't part of The Plan. If Mom caves in, her follow-through goes out the window—and

> *Without follow-through all you have is the talk without the walk.*

Mitch and Ryan may decide that pushing Mom's buttons sometimes gets them what they want. Consistently kind and firm follow-through shows respect for Mom and the needs of the situation and respect for the boys. Follow-through makes the pitch in baseball and makes the point in discipline. Without follow-through all you have is the talk without the walk.

What should you do if you say or do something you want to "take back" after you think about it awhile? By no means make two wrongs from one! Instead, share your mistake with your children. You won't appear foolish if you apologize for something you wish you hadn't said or done. Your children need to know you make mistakes too, and that once the mistake is recognized, you are prepared to make restitution for your error.

Positive Discipline Tools in the Real World

Remember the Mistaken Goal Chart from Chapter 7? The final column lists proactive and empowering responses for you to choose when your child misbehaves. Let's take a look at what those responses might look like in a real life situation after we first remember a few thoughts to keep in mind:

1. Parents must make the first steps of change; the child will follow.
2. Things *may* get worse through a period of testing before they get better.
3. Discipline is teaching, not punishment.
4. Parenting is a job for a lifetime rather than one you will do for a short time, or one time only.
5. Children *do* better when they *feel* better, so discipline will be most effective when it is both kind *and* firm.
6. You will always need a variety of parenting tools; no tool works every time for all families.

Remember to listen to your common sense, and to seek guidance from the Lord whenever possible. Your knowledge of your own child and your inner wisdom will help you know which tool is the right tool for each situation. Let's look at a common event in most families—the power struggle—to see what the Positive Discipline tools look like in real life.

Misguided Power and Your Parenting Toolbox

Seventeen-year-old Tricia has decided that her high-school curfew is cramping her style now that she has graduated. After all, she's heading off to college pretty soon, and she doesn't plan to call her parents then. When Tricia entered adolescence and began to spend more time with her friends, she and her parents had agreed to set her curfew based on her plans. If she was going to be later than agreed, she could call or text the details of the need for a curfew adjustment. Her communication (before the time she was due home) would be honored if there was a reason that her parents could understand, such as "the pizza just arrived' or "I've got to take George home first, and the movie let out later than we'd planned."

Tricia had always agreed to do an extra job the next day to help out Mom or Dad or to come in earlier the next night should she "forget" to call and negotiate. Because Tricia and her family agreed it was important to know where family members were and how they could be reached, everyone in the family left notes, texted each other, or called home when plans changed. They agreed this was a mutually respectful thing to do, and no one had ever challenged this rule—at least intentionally.

Tonight seemed different, somehow. Tricia hadn't called home, though she had agreed she would be home by 12:30 a.m., right after the late show let out. No call—and it was now 1:15 a.m. Where could she be? This was the third time in less than a week that Tricia had pulled a similar stunt. Her parents were angry and feeling somewhat defeated (and they were worried about their daughter's safety). "Our limits are kind *and* firm," they said. "We discussed this curfew thing together, and we all agreed on the importance of this family rule. Why is Tricia testing our patience like this?"

What can Tricia's parents do? Turn to your Mistaken Goal Chart. There is always more than one tool possible that meets the Five Criteria for Positive Discipline. Read through Column 7 for effective ways to handle this example of "misguided power." Here are three creatively blended solutions for Tricia's parents to consider:

1. Redirect to Positive Power by Asking for Help; Encourage:

Tricia's parents could ask her to help them understand why she has been late three times in the last week, as this has never been a problem throughout high school. "Tricia, I'm having a hard time understanding why you've been late three times this week. That's more than you were late your whole senior year! What's going on?"

2. Don't Fight and Don't Give In; Withdraw from Conflict; Be Firm and Kind; Decide What You Will Do; Leave and Calm Down; Develop Mutual Respect; Use Family Meetings; Encourage; Practice Follow-Through:

Tricia's parents could say to Tricia when she arrives home, "We'll talk about this in the morning when we are all fresh. We want to listen to you, rather than argue with you, and we are feeling too angry now to do that. We're glad you are safe, as this is our biggest worry." In the morning, Tricia will be more ready to talk about her mistaken belief that calling home doesn't matter anymore. Her parents may be able to better understand her feelings and her mistaken, underlying belief that she is seventeen and grown-up enough not to call home with her every move.

3. Develop Mutual Respect; Encourage; Offer Limited Choices; Set a Few Reasonable Limits; Decide What You Will Do; Let Routines Be Boss; Practice Follow-Through:

Tricia's parents could say, "Here are some choices we can think of that will help us get along this summer. You may take one of these choices about going out, Tricia:

a. We can make one curfew time that is standard and not negotiable.

b. You can negotiate the time you need by calling/texting us by 11 p.m. Should you decide not to contact us by 11 p.m., we will be expecting you to be home by 12:30 a.m. If you decide not to contact us and not be home by 12:30 a.m., what do you think would help you remember our agreement? It isn't okay to be late without calling. Your Mom and I are still working on the weekdays, and we need our rest. We're willing to work with you, but we can't go to bed and relax when we are worrying about where you are."

What would you do if you were Tricia's parents? Again, there is no one "right" answer to this question. Parents often get in the locked-horns position with their children, believing that they are sacrificing their parental authority if they don't win over their children. (Do they really want their children to be the "losers"?) Yet, being disrespectful to the child who is expressing power in unacceptable ways will not help either parent or child in the short (or the long) run. When tempers seethe about "who is right," parents may speak more through body language and emotional reactions than from the heart.

Take time to cool down when you need it. Tricia's parents used their own emotions to uncover her mistaken goal: *I belong only when I'm the boss, in control; no one can boss me… you can't make me.* By choosing to communicate with dignity and respect, even though feelings of anger were strongly brewing, Tricia's parents revealed their maturity and patience.

In Romans 7: 21-23, Paul shows us how difficult this is, even for him: "So I find this law at work: When I want to do good, evil is right there with me. For in my inner being I delight in God's law; but I see another law at work in the members of my body, waging war against the law of my mind and making me a prisoner of the law of sin at work within my members."

It is important for parents to deal with their understandable—but potentially harmful—anger in constructive ways. How parents handle anger imprints a developing child's emotional map forever. Proverbs 18: 21 tells us: "The tongue has the power of life and death, and those who love it will eat its fruit." What parents say and do in anger or frustration can haunt parent-child relationships forever, or can become the foundation upon which children can build self-control, responsibility, and conflict-resolution skills. James 1:19-20 warns us to take heed to follow the more difficult path: "My dear brothers, take note of this: Everyone should be quick to listen, slow to speak and slow to become angry, for man's anger does not bring about the righteous life that God desires."

> What parents say and do in anger or frustration can haunt parent-child relationships forever, or can become the foundation upon which children can build self-control, responsibility, and conflict-resolution skills.

A person of faith knows God's grace is His power released through love. Dropping the power struggle did *not* mean that Tricia would win and her parents would lose. On the contrary, when parents keep their eyes on the issue and their hearts in the Lord, they become channels of God's power to their children, letting His power guide their actions and speech. God will show the parent and child who seek Him during family conflicts the gentle grace to do what is right for the situation.

Summary

The following list of Positive Discipline Attitude and Action Tools contains tools of respectful instruction rather than tools for spiteful destruction. Betty and Joe, the couple you met at the beginning of this chapter, received a handout with these tools in the parenting class they took at their church. From yelling, nagging, and exasperation they've moved to firmness, kindness, and encouragement. Before, their parenting toolbox was almost empty; now they have a toolbox full of empowering choices—and so do you! You might want to keep this list, the Mistaken Goal Chart, and your growing list of helpful Scripture verses close by for frequent reference. (Usually the fridge is the household's busiest bulletin board!)

In Proverbs 17:6 we read a summary of what the whole book of Proverbs implies: parents and children are not meant to be adversaries, but allies in life who are proud of each other. (Compton's Interactive Bible) These tools can help you and your children work together to a build a loving and respectful family.

FOURTEEN ATTITUDE TOOLS

1. Children's primary goal is to experience belonging and significance. Misbehaving children are discouraged children.

2. "Where did we ever get the crazy idea that in order to get children to do better, first we have to make them feel worse? Children *do* better when they *feel* better."

3. Mistakes are wonderful opportunities to learn.

4. Work for improvement, not perfection.

5. Use kindness and firmness at the same time.

6. Focus on winning children over instead of winning over children.

7. Beware of what works. Focus on long-range results—teaching children valuable characteristics and life skills.

8. Are you looking for blame or are you looking for solutions?

9. Understand the meaning of discipline.

10. Positive discipline is based on treating children with dignity and respect.

11. Children listen to you *after* they feel listened to.

12. Learn to understand the code for the hidden message behind misbehavior.

13. Give children the benefit of the doubt.

14. Lighten up—breathe.

Reference: Jane Nelsen, *Positive Time-Out and Over 50 Ways to Avoid Power Struggles in Homes and Classrooms*, Jane Nelsen, Ed. D., 1999, Three Rivers Press.

FORTY-TWO ACTION TOOLS
(for Avoiding Power Struggles While Empowering Children)

As you become familiar with these action tools, you will notice that many of them work best when combined with another tool. And of course, they will be more effective when combined with the fourteen attitude tools. That's why we listed the attitude tools first!

None of these tools work all the time for every problem and with every child. Whenever you find yourself involved in a power struggle or in any kind of conflict with your children, take some time out and go over these action and attitude tools. One (or several) may seem just right for you and for your children.

1. Make sure the message of love and respect gets through

2. Create opportunities for children to develop Significant Seven Perceptions and Skills

3. Don't do things for children that they can do for themselves

4. Ask what and how questions

5. Use curiosity questions

6. Get children involved in solutions

7. Have regular family meetings

8. One-on-one problem solving between two young people

9. Create routines *with* children

10. Offer limited choices

11. Redirect misguided power

12. "I notice"

13. Focus on solutions (during family meetings or one-on-one or anytime)

14. Create a "Wheel of Choice"

15. Emotional honesty: "I feel ____ about/when ____ because ____ and I wish _____"

16. Teach children the difference between what they feel and what they do

17. Take responsibility for your part in the conflict

18. Give them a timer to set themselves

19. Get into your child's world; deal with the belief behind the behavior

20. Active listening

21. Supervision, supervision, supervision

22. Distract and/or redirect

23. Use the 4 R's of recovery from mistakes

24. Stay out of fights

25. Put them in the same boat ... Treat them the same

26. Take time for training

27. Decide what you will do

28. Follow through

29. Shut your mouth and act

30. Less is more

31. Use nonverbal signals when emotions are high

32. As soon as _____ then _____

33. Natural consequences

34. Logical consequences

35. Opportunity = Responsibility = Consequence

36. Use encouragement instead of praise or rewards

37. Allowances not related to chores

38. Get children involved in chores

39. Hugs

40. Special time

41. Positive time out

42. And, again, make sure the message of love and respect gets through

Reference: Jane Nelsen, *Positive Time-Out and Over 50 Ways to Avoid Power Struggles in Homes and Classrooms*, Jane Nelsen, Ed. D., 1999, Three Rivers Press.

Chapter 9

The Magic of Encouragement

"Therefore encourage one another, and build each other up."

(1 Thessalonians 5:11)

Dora and Cindy Shelton were raised by an excessively strict, harshly critical, and emotionally distant dad and a timid, fearful mom. Just a year and a half apart in age, they might have been the best of friends, but they reacted very differently to their dad's criticism and grew into polar opposites. Dora, the older, "lived down" to his criticism, becoming precisely the young woman he predicted. Her life became a series of ongoing battles with those in positions of authority, and she spent most of her young adult years in and out of various substance abuse programs. An adult now, she is drifting aimlessly through life with little self-confidence and less joy.

Cindy, on the other hand, "lived up" to her dad's criticisms, continuously striving to be the perfect child, consistently doing what she was told at home, always bringing home straight A's, and never coming to the breakfast table without having first made her bed. Today she is a successful corporate executive, well-known in business circles for her demanding style and for getting things done. Sadly, she is also several times divorced and alienated from her three children.

Many of us were taught that love requires that we faithfully point out the shortcomings of our children. If they are to grow in wisdom and grace, then we must be vigilant in catching them when they do wrong, criticizing them, and punishing them for their failings. Dora and Cindy's dad certainly thought so. He believed that he was offering only "constructive criticism"; he was a good man who criticized his children so that they would become better people. It was certainly not his intent that they grow into adults with serious relationship difficulties. It was not his intent that they lead lives of discouragement, rebelling against authority (like Dora) or embracing authority a little too much and alienating yet another generation (like Cindy). But criticism, no matter how it is intended, is still criticism. Dad did not intend to discourage his daughters—but he did. The opposite of dis-couragement is en-couragement. The apostle Paul instructs us to "encourage one another and build each other up." (1 Thessalonians 5:11) And he tells us why: "God did not appoint us to suffer wrath, but to receive salvation through our Lord Jesus Christ." (1 Thessalonians 5:9) God sees our goodness (not only our sins and mistakes) and wishes for us his ultimate gift, eternal salvation. He wants us to be en-couraged, not dis-couraged. And He wants us to be encouraging to others. What a wonderful model for parenthood!

Rudolf Dreikurs, in *Children: The Challenge,* writes that "encouragement is more important than any other aspect of child-raising. It is so important that the lack of it can be considered the basic cause for misbehavior. "A misbehaving child is a discouraged child," Dreikurs said, and compared encouragement for a child to water for a plant. Without it, they both die, one physically, the other emotionally.

It might be hard to see that the rebellious child standing in front of you—arms folded across her chest, defiant look in her eyes, adamantly refusing to pick up her toys—is discouraged. She looks pretty much in control of things, doesn't she? If anyone is discouraged, you're probably thinking, it's *Mom*, not this seven-year-old child insisting on her own way.

But this child *is* discouraged. She is discouraged because she senses that she has no power, no ability to influence things, and, therefore, no sense of belonging or significance in the family. In her eyes, life is a long series of lectures and commands from Mom; to claim her sense of belonging and significance, she must exert her power whenever possible. (Remember, too, that autonomy and initiative are normal developmental stages through which all children and teens pass. Parents who invite power struggles with these children will find them willing participants.) When a child does not receive guidance in how to use her power effectively, she will use it indiscriminately and in increasingly unhealthy ways.

If this child had come up to Mom and innocently said, "I am a child and I just want to belong," Mom would have embraced her. Believe it or not, that is what she is saying, in her own inarticulate way. Behavior is a child's way of speaking to parents in "code"—the phrase "acting out" is actually quite accurate, as misbehavior is a child's way of acting out her discouragement. That defiant "No!" is her way of saying, "I believe that the only way I can have power is to defy my parents. I believe that mom and dad are always telling me what to do and when to do it. I don't feel that I belong—at least, not right now. Please understand that I am a child and I just want to belong."

"Well," you might be saying, "parents are *supposed* to be the authorities in the family. They're supposed to discipline and teach children, and show them what to do." But as we will learn, there are ways of teaching and training children that encourage them, and that invite them to work *with* parents and teachers instead of against them.

Encouragement—the ability to build on strengths, to notice what is right, and to build a sense of belonging and significance—is one of the most powerful parenting tools you will ever discover. Human beings almost always do better when they feel better; believing you are worthwhile—that you can make a positive contribution and are appreciated as the unique person God created—encourages you to do your best in life. When parents can learn to replace discouragement with encouragement, their children will be less likely to misbehave, and may even discover the joy in cooperation and contribution. (Well, at least most of the time: after all, no one is perfect!) Parents sometimes struggle with the idea that children can have power, but each person, including the child, has real personal power. You really can't "give" it to them (because they already have it), nor can you take it away from them. You can only help them redirect it, and learn to use it in positive ways.

How can parents replace discouragement with encouragement? Many parents are in the habit of reacting to misbehavior in negative ways (in ways, perhaps, that they learned from their own parents). It takes time, patience, and practice to discover and accept the belief *behind* behavior, and to deal with the hidden message—"I am a child, and I just want to belong"—that lies just behind that defiant "No!" Many parents punish their children in the hope that the unpleasant punishment will change the behavior. But punishment does not address the hidden message, and the child remains discouraged. Punishment may change behavior in the short term, but the goal of finding belonging and significance has not been addressed. The defiance will return. Many parents mistakenly believe that the way to encourage children and create a sense of belonging is by offering lots of praise and rewards. Unfortunately, praise and rewards are actually discouraging to children in the long term. We will discuss this later in the chapter.

> Encouragement—the ability to build on strengths, to notice what is right, and to build a sense of belonging and significance—is one of the most powerful parenting tools you will ever discover.

How can parents encourage the child who continually and

stubbornly says "No"? Given the high emotional charge of the encounter—parents are deeply frustrated and may believe their authority is being challenged, while the child is angry and defiant—it is probably best to take a positive time out (see Chapter 8) rather than attempting to solve the problem "right now." Time—and a little space apart—can work wonders. You could, for example, say, "It looks like neither one of us is in a position to deal with this respectfully right now. Let's talk about this after dinner when we're both in a better mood." After dinner, with the emotions safely in check, you could use the Four Steps for Winning Cooperation to help create a more encouraging atmosphere for problem solving.

The Four Steps for Winning Cooperation

Has your spouse ever paused, in the middle of an argument, and said, "You know, I think I understand your point"? If so, did you almost immediately feel a sense of acceptance, of encouragement? It's the same with children—just knowing that Mom or Dad understands their perspective goes a long way toward defusing the problem.

That's the point of the Four Steps for Winning Cooperation:

- **Express understanding for how you think your child is feeling.** Be sure to check with her to see if you are right. "Could it be that you would like to pick up your toys later on rather than right now?" (You might want to use active listening, which we will explore in Chapter 10 on communication and feelings.)
- **Show understanding of the child's perception.** This doesn't mean that you necessarily agree with the child, just that you understand how she is seeing the problem. It may help to share a time when you felt or behaved similarly. "I can understand that. My mom used to tell me to clean my room up immediately, and all I wanted to do was keep playing."
- **Share your own feelings and perceptions.** If the first two steps have been done with sincerity and friendliness, the child will be more willing to listen. "I really appreciate it when everyone in the family cleans up after themselves. I like the house to look nice and I think you do, too."
- **Ask the child if she would be willing to work on a solution together.** "Can you think of any ways that we could solve this problem together so you can play with your toys and put them away when you're finished?" The child will probably come up with some ideas of her own, but if she's stuck, you can make suggestions, preferably in a way that continues to involve the child in the decision. "Something I remember doing when I was young was playing with my toys in the family room and agreeing to put them all away before dinner was served. Perhaps you could keep your favorite toys in a box in the family room; that would make clean-up easier."

FOUR STEPS TO WINNING COOPERATION

1. Express understanding for how you think your child is feeling

2. Show understanding of the child's perception

3. Share your own feelings and perceptions

4. Ask the child if she would be willing to work on a solution together

---

These Four Steps to Winning Cooperation may seem cold and clinical, but when you can personalize them and take them to heart, they work wonders. The most important ingredient is your willingness to show understanding for your child's perceptions. Just as we appreciate it when our spouse expresses understanding of how we feel, so too do our children.

Respect

Key to the success of the Four Steps to Winning Cooperation is respect. Respect is best taught by modeling, by treating yourself and others with respect every day of your lives together. When you can get down on one knee to make eye contact, respectfully show understanding of your child's feelings and perceptions, and then work together toward a solution, so much more is possible than when you fall back on, "Do it now!"

Talking about being respectful and actually practicing respect with children are two very different things. By the way, showing respect for children does not mean giving them adult privileges or responsibilities; it simply means respecting the humanity and spirit of each child, something Jesus modeled when he told his disciples to allow the children to come and sit near him. Most parents intend to speak with respectfulness but somehow those old, disrespectful words (the ones you may have heard during your own childhood) just pop out.

One key to practicing mutual respect is to learn the *language* of respect. Mike, one of the authors, is a former school principal who once asked his students to identify the expressions that they most hate to hear their parents say. The top five most hated expressions—the "Five Forbidden Phrases"—are:

1. "What part of 'no' don't you understand?"
2. "When I was your age . . ."
3. "If everyone else jumped off the cliff, would you do the same?"
4. "No one ever said life is fair." and
5. "Because I said so."

Note that each expression conveys sarcasm and/or authoritarianism, two disrespectful (and ultimately ineffective) ways of dealing with others. When Mike does workshops on the Five Forbidden Phrases, he helps participants "overwrite" their old scripts with new, more respectful scripts. For example, instead of "Because I said so," you can practice saying, "Because it's the right thing to do," which is respectful and which teaches that we are all subject to a higher authority from whom we learn the difference between right and wrong. As the Bible tells us, "This is how we know that we love the children of God: by loving God and carrying out his commandments. This is love for God: to obey his commands. And his commands are not burdensome." (1 John 5:2-3)

The Magic of Encouragement

There is a story about the Babema tribe in South Africa that practices a unique approach to solving disciplinary matters among its members. In this particular tribe, when a person acts irresponsibly or unjustly he is placed in the center of the village, alone but unrestrained. All work ceases in the village, and every man, woman, and child gathers in a large circle around the accused individual.

Then each person in the tribe begins to talk out loud to the accused, one at a time, about all the good things the accused has done in his lifetime. Every incident and every experience that can be recalled with any detail and accuracy is recounted. All the positive attributes, all the good deeds, all the strengths and kindness that the accused has given to the village over the years are recited at great length. No one fabricates or exaggerates about the person's accomplishments or the positive aspects of his personality. They simply speak the truth.

The tribal ceremony can last for an entire day, and does not cease until everyone has made every possible comment he can about the accused. At the end, the tribal circle is broken, a joyous celebration takes place, and the person is symbolically and literally welcomed back into the tribe. Imagine how that person must feel as he hears these words of encouragement from his friends and family; imagine how your child might feel if you could speak such words to her.

This beautiful story illustrates the magic of encouragement in helping our children do better. Encouragement is welcoming and strengthening, and it enhances rather than harms the relationships among us. Punishment and criticism weaken our relationships, sometimes permanently. Imagine how our children would feel if we offered them reminders of all the good things they have done instead of criticizing them when they do wrong.

Jesus and the Woman Caught in Adultery

There is perhaps no better example of encouragement than that of Jesus with the woman caught in adultery (John 8: 1-11). Sitting in the temple area in Jerusalem, Jesus was teaching the people who had come to hear Him. In the middle of this peaceful scene, the Scribes and Pharisees arrived, dragging a woman who had been caught in adultery. They challenged Jesus, knowing that He preaches forgiveness rather than condemnation: "Teacher, this woman was caught in the very act of adultery . . . Moses commanded us to stone such women. So what do you say?"

Jesus did not answer them but, instead, began to write in the sand. There has been much speculation about what Jesus wrote in the sand that day. We will never know (in this world, anyway). But some suggest that He was writing down the sins of this woman's accusers. Could He have been writing all the positive qualities of this woman, or all the good deeds she had done? Or perhaps He was writing down the two great commandments, to love God and to love one another. Maybe He was reminding the Scribes and Pharisees of the words He spoke in the Sermon on the Mount, "blessed are the merciful, for they will be shown mercy." (Matthew 5:7) We do not know.

What we do know is that Jesus' words in the sand did not stop the woman's accusers and so He rose and said to them: "Let the one among you who is without sin cast the first stone," Jesus returned to His writing in the sand. And one by one, the accusers left. As we saw earlier, Jesus did not condone her sin, but he did not punish her. Instead, he encouraged her to begin a new life.

> *Encouragement is welcoming and strengthening, and it enhances rather than harms the relationships among us.*

Reframing and Redirecting Misbehavior

Your efforts to encourage your children will probably never have the drama of Jesus and the woman caught in adultery, but there are many small ways to encourage them through love and respect. One helpful exercise for parents is to reframe a behavior seen as a negative characteristic into a positive characteristic. You can choose to look on the bright side: the same "stubbornness" in your son that so annoys you today may, with love and guidance, become the perseverance and confidence that allows him to make good choices, resist negative peer pressure, and enjoy a successful life as a teenager or adult.

Reframing is an attitude; redirecting is an action. When you reframe, you make the effort to see your children in a different light. On one level, your child is stubborn. But on a higher level, he is strong in his values, and for that you may choose to feel gratitude.

When you redirect, you put reframing into action by giving your children opportunities to see themselves differently. Giving a "bossy" child special responsibilities "because I know I can always count on you to get things done" teaches the child that the same character trait can be used in positive or negative ways. It has been said that attitude is everything. If you look for the positive qualities your children possess, you will certainly find them.

Looking for Improvement, Not Perfection

Mark Twain once wrote about a preacher he heard who, by the close of his sermon, had reduced the number of the elect to "a number so small it was hardly worth the saving." That was not Jesus' way; although He sets high standards for us, He is always ready to forgive us and to encourage us to sin no more. In our interactions with our own children, it is usually wise to follow Jesus' example and not that of Mark Twain's preacher.

In the story that opened this chapter, we read about a dad who thought it was his responsibility to point out each of his daughters' failings, in the hope that his "helpful" criticism would make them better people. It didn't work for him, and it won't work for us. Expecting perfection will result in very discouraged children (and very frustrated parents). It is far more encouraging (and effective) to notice effort and improvement: "Thanks for picking up your room. It looks so much better, and I appreciate your help."

If you "fix" your child's work, or immediately point out all the items that were missed, what will she be deciding? She may decide, "Nothing I do satisfies Mom and Dad; I may as well give up." Or "The only way to find love and belonging in this family is to do everything perfectly." Neither decision is likely to create a competent, confident child or encourage cooperation. Notice effort; show genuine appreciation for what your child *does* do. Remember, children usually *do* better when they *feel* better.

Dealing with Social Pressure

Parents often say that one of the hardest things they face in raising their children as Christians is social pressure. When your children ask you if they can go to a movie that you find objectionable (assuring you, of course, that everyone *else's* parents said it was okay), it is often difficult to say no with kindness and firmness. Parents sometimes revert to one of the Five Forbidden Phrases— "Because I said so!"—to bolster their argument.

As Christians, we have no need to resort to "because I said so." We have a higher authority, Jesus Himself, who gave us a standard of behavior in the New Testament. "What Would Jesus Do" may have become overly popularized in recent years, but there is much in those simple words that can guide our daily decisions.

When your child wants to follow the crowd or test your family boundaries, you can choose to make that moment an opportunity for encouragement and teaching. What is it about your child's request that troubles you? What do you want him to think, to feel, and to decide? Is there a way to encourage cooperation, rather than inviting a power struggle? And how does this issue reflect your faith? What, indeed, would Jesus do? Taking time to teach is one of the most encouraging things a parent can do for a child.

Special Time

Have you ever had a teacher take you aside and, with no one else around, tell you that you did a great job on a project or that your contribution to class was particularly insightful today, or thank you for helping out with a task after school? Or perhaps you had a teacher who took time to talk about problems with you. If so, it's probably a memory that will stick with you forever. The special, one-on-one time that an adult gives to a child is rarely forgotten.

> Allow each of your children to see their "special-ness" in your eyes as you provide them that daily, one-on-one, undivided attention.

Most of us can vividly remember some special one-on-one time with our parents. (And if we can't, we usually wish we could.) Perhaps it was when Dad read to us our favorite story—over and over and over again! Perhaps it was Mom's special time with us just before lights out. Or that camping trip—just Dad and me! There is true magic in those moments. Look for those special, one-on-one opportunities. Make them a part of your daily rituals. Allow each of your children to see their "special-ness" in your eyes as you provide them that daily, one-on-one, undivided attention. Let them know they belong in the family and that they are worthy of your time and attention.

Encouragement and Praise

Everyone knows about the importance of praise. Parents everywhere have "One Hundred Ways to Praise a Child" posted on their refrigerators; they offer praise about their child's every action, post art work on every available wall, and believe that in doing so, they are building their child's self-esteem. But praise—especially praise that is insincere or overdone—can lead children to become people-pleasers and approval-junkies, people who believe they are acceptable only when someone else is telling them they are.

Shannon's Mom and Dad had looked forward to her first day at kindergarten for an entire year. Mom had told Shannon at least a hundred times, "Remember, dear, always do what the teacher says. Always smile and always make sure your hair is just right. And don't get your dress dirty . . ." and on and on and on. So Shannon did what her mom told her. Shannon, in fact, became the consummate people-pleaser, and, predictably, her teachers loved her.

But sometime early in her sixth grade year, Shannon discovered that she was no longer getting the same responses from the significant people in her life from her adult-pleasing ways. It wasn't that the adults were no longer pleased with her; Shannon had, as children do, begun to care more about what her peers thought of her than what her parents and teachers thought. Gradually, she began to do things that earned the admiration of her fellow students. Unfortunately, these were not things her parents approved of. Shannon became more and more popular as she moved into middle school and high school, but her grades and behavior began to suffer. She argued with her parents and felt guilty about her behavior. Shannon became increasingly discouraged.

Encouragement, as the word suggests, is the effort to inspire a child with courage, the courage to do the right thing whether or not Mom, Dad, or the teacher is looking. Remember our discussion of the root word in encouragement in Chapter 8? The root word of "courage" is the French word "coeur," or heart. En-courage actually means "to give heart to." Dis-courage is "taking heart away from." The child who is encouraged is the child who has developed the internal courage to make decisions because they are the right decisions, a character quality also known as integrity. Isn't this what parents want for their children as they come face to face with the many temptations the world places before them?

Praise looks to the person—"You are such a good girl for cleaning your room." Encouragement looks to the effort—"I can tell that you worked very hard at organizing your room. Thank you—you must feel good about that." Praise looks to the number of A's on the report card. Encouragement looks to what was learned. Praise leads to dependence on others. Encouragement leads to self-confidence, self-reliance, and, ultimately, true self-esteem.

Parents sometimes believe that they can "give" self-esteem through praise, but as we have learned, this sometimes backfires. Self-esteem actually grows out of life skills, what are sometimes called "competency experiences." Can you remember a time when your child tried something new—perhaps snowboarding, gymnastics, or cooking a meal—and succeeded at it? How did he feel? One of the hidden blessings of inviting children to share responsibilities and teaching them the skills to do so is that you are building their own sense of confidence and competence in a way mere words never can. Self-esteem cannot be "given"; it must be grown within the heart of each child.

The encouraged Christian (both young and old) will make choices about life and relationships based on his or her belief that those choices are the right ones to make. The Christian who has been raised to expect praise for doing the right thing will become confused and discouraged when the choices he or she makes are not met with praise.

Rewards

Rewards teach a child to respond to an "external locus of control." In other words, a child learns to do things only because there is a reward. This makes the parent responsible for the child's behavior—not the child. This, then is the parent's job: to "catch" kids being good so he can dole out the rewards and to "catch" kids being bad so he can mete out earned punishment. One of the foundational principles of Positive Discipline is that a child should learn to do the right thing simply because it *is* the right thing—for the "intrinsic" or internal knowing that one has contributed to family, community, or society. Conventional wisdom teaches that rewards are the best motivators to help children do better. And rewards really *do* work—if all you are interested in is the short-term results. However, sometimes you must "beware of what works" because of the long-term results. Many children will be motivated by rewards for a while. However, they may soon want bigger and better rewards, or refuse to do the task at all.

It is usually better to teach children self-discipline and cooperation rather than dependence on you for rewards or punishment.

Differences between Praise and Encouragement

	Praise	Encouragement
Dictionary Definition	1. To express a favorable judgment of 2. To glorify, especially by attribution of perfection 3. An expression of approval	1. To inspire with courage 2. To spur on; stimulate
Recognizes	Only complete perfect product	Effort and improvement
Attitude	Patronizing; manipulative	Respectful; appreciative
"I" Message	Judgmental; "I like the way you are sitting…"	Self-disclosing: "I appreciate your cooperation"
Used most often with	Children: "You're such a good little girl"	Adults: "Thanks for helping"
Examples	"I'm proud of you for getting an A in math" (Robs the person of ownership of a personal achievement)	"That A reflects your hard work" (Recognizes ownership and responsibility for the achievement)
Invites	People to change for others	People to change for themselves
Locus of Control	External: "What do you think?"	Internal: "What do I think?"
Teaches	What to think, based on what others think	How to Think
Goal	Conformity:"You did it right"	Understanding: "What do you think/feel?"
Effect on Self-Esteem	Feel worthwhile only when others approve	Feel worthwhile without approval of others
Long-Range Effect	Dependence on others	Self-confidence, self-reliance and independent worth

* This is based on a chart by parenting educators and parenting class leaders Bonnie G. Smith and Judy Dixon, of Sacramento, California.

Tools to Encourage Our Children

Here are some tips for ways you can encourage your children every day, thereby fostering self-confidence and self-esteem.

Take Time for Training

We are all familiar with Proverbs (22:6). But have we stopped to think about what the word training really means? Do we take time for training, or do we just assume that our children understand what we want them to do?

Consider the story of Marian. Marian's mother included her in as many household activities as possible when she was growing up. One of her earliest memories is of doing the family wash with her mother. Although Marian was only three years old, her memory of working alongside her mother remains vivid. Mom's job was to take the wet clothes out of the washing machine and hand them to Marian, waiting expectantly next to her. Marian would then place the pile of wet clothes in the dryer, close the door tightly, press the start button, and stand back in pride for a job well done. Growing up, Marian was convinced that it took two to do the family wash. Mom had taken time to teach Marian how to do a small part of the housework, but Marian never forgot it—and learned some valuable life lessons because of it.

> The task for parents is to build on those strengths little by little, while helping children learn to manage their inevitable weaknesses.

Young children often ask, "Mommy, let me help." At that point—a powerful teaching opportunity each time it occurs—you can teach one of two lessons: "You're too little to help; go play with your toys." Or like Marian's mom, you can say, "I'd really appreciate your help. Let me show you how to operate the dryer." Parents often miss opportunities to involve children when they truly *want* to be involved, dismissing their efforts because they are "too young," or because training them and encouraging them takes time parents may not believe they have. Then, when children are older, those same parents wonder why they refuse to help and only want to play with their toys. Investing your time and energy in teaching your children will benefit all of you for years to come.

Build on Strengths; Manage Weaknesses

God made us all different, with different strengths and different weaknesses. As Paul points out in 1 Corinthians 12, to some God gave particular gifts, and to others He gave other gifts; they are all the work of the same Spirit. We all know these familiar words, yet we sometimes forget how this applies to raising children. Each of our children has unique gifts and strengths. The task for parents is to build on those strengths little by little, while helping children learn to manage their inevitable weaknesses.

The first step, of course, is to discover just what your child's strengths are. We like the concept advocated by Tom J. Peters in his book, *In Search of Excellence* (Harper Business Essentials, 2004). Be a "good finder," Peters advocates. Look for what is working, recognize it, and in so doing, be an encourager to those around you. Peters is writing about encouragement in the business world, but it is perhaps even more important for parents! Be a good finder and, amazingly, the good will be found . . . and it will increase because what we focus on increases.

Ask Questions Instead of Issuing Orders

Jesus had a knack for asking questions in a way that gave the listener an opportunity to understand what He was teaching. Can you hear the invitation and encouragement in the following questions?

- "Who among you is without sin?"
- "Which is easier to say, 'Your sins are forgiven', or 'rise and walk'?"
- "Which one of you who has a sheep that falls into a pit on the Sabbath will not take hold of it and lift it out?"

When you ask open-ended questions of your children instead of giving commands, you are far more likely to receive cheerful cooperation than when you command, direct, and expect. (How do you feel when others order you around? Are you inspired to cooperate, or do you feel just a little resentful?) "There's lots of work to do today. What can you do to help me?" is much more encouraging than "This is what you will do today."

Asking children how they can help us gives them an opportunity to contribute, and when they contribute they develop a sense of belonging, connection, contribution, and significance in the family.

Have the Courage to Be Imperfect

As we have suggested from time to time in this book, perfection is outside our grasp (so long as we are on this side of the grave). So we might as well come to terms with the fact that we are going to make mistakes. And so will our children.

Wouldn't it be wonderful if we could say to our child, who has just broken a plate while clearing the table, "That's okay. We all make mistakes. What can you learn from this?" Or even better: "Whoops! I made a mistake in not showing you how to clear the table. Let's talk about what you're doing and see if we can come up with a better plan."

When Paul said, "Fathers, do not provoke your children, so they may not become discouraged" (Colossians 3:21, NKJV), he was reminding us that we need to give children room to be imperfect, too, and time to learn all the skills and attitudes they will need to be successful, happy people. Paul tells us, "You do not need to be a perfect parent. And your children will not be perfect, either. Cut them some slack. After all, it is only through our mistakes that we learn."

> *When you ask open-ended questions of your children instead of giving commands, you are far more likely to receive cheerful cooperation than when you command, direct, and expect.*

Have you ever misjudged your child, perhaps accusing him of doing something wrong, only to find out that it was *you* who were wrong? Did you apologize to your child? Most parents discover that when they are humble enough to accept responsibility for their own mistakes and offer a sincere apology, their children are quick to forgive.

The authors know a great deal about being imperfect: we've been doing it for years, as our children can attest only too well. Mary shares a story about her own courage to be imperfect. Mary and her family had just moved into a new home when Mary discovered a deep, fresh scratch on her shiny kitchen counter.

"Okay, kids, get in here!" she yelled. "Can't you remember you're supposed to use the cutting board? Now, who did it?"

All three children responded with a chorus of, "Not me! I didn't do it!"

Mary, however, was not impressed. "All right," she said firmly, "we'll just stand here until one of you admits it." Mary set the timer for two minutes: more shouts of "I didn't do it!" followed. She set the timer for three minutes, with the same result, then four minutes. Ten minutes of silence later, the telephone rang. It was Gary, Mary's husband, calling from work.

Mary shared her frustration about the scratched counter, and told her husband that she was waiting for one of the children to confess. "It's been ten minutes," Mary moaned, "and they still won't tell me who did it."

There was a long silence on the other end of the telephone line. Then Gary said quietly, "I did it. I was cutting out coupons and got a little carried away."

TOOLS FOR ENCOURAGING YOUR CHILD

- Take time for training
- Build on strengths; manage weaknesses
- Ask questions instead of issuing orders
- Have the courage to be imperfect

Needless to say, Mary had a bit of pride to swallow. She apologized to her three children—who forgave her instantly and offered hugs. The family still laughs about the time Mom tried to "just get the truth."

Children are so forgiving, as quick to offer encouragement as they are glad to receive it. Have the courage to be imperfect and to model humility with your children, and to offer forgiveness for their mistakes. "Bear with each other and forgive whatever grievances you may have against one another. Forgive as the Lord forgave you. And over all these virtues put on love, which binds them all together in perfect unity." (Colossians 3:13-14) Imagine what welcoming, encouraging places our homes might become if we practiced respect, encouragement, and forgiveness each and every day.

Have the courage to be imperfect, to model humility with your children, and to offer forgiveness for their mistakes.

Chapter 10

"A Gentle Answer Turns Away Wrath": Understanding Feelings and Communication

One of the first verses a child learns is Psalm118:24, "This is the day the Lord has made; let us rejoice and be glad in it." In fact, the Bible is filled with Scriptures that speak of joy and gladness. Why is it, then, that Christians still struggle with sadness, anxiety, fear, and anger? Why can't our families—and, indeed, the world outside our homes—be joyous and peaceful all of the time?

Well, one simple answer is that the Lord in His wisdom made us with a full spectrum of emotions. Much like the rainbow that follows the rain, some have speculated that we would not fully appreciate happy times if we did not experience sad times. Remember how much you appreciated your health after being sick? In fact, your feelings are intended to give you valuable information about yourself and the world around you. Feelings are your barometer: They keep you tuned in to what's happening, and often give you clues about what you need to do to stay safe and healthy.

Children, too, have strong emotions. Their feelings are just as powerful (and occasionally, just as overwhelming) as those of the adults around them, but they usually have fewer words to describe their emotions (and fewer skills to help them manage emotions) than do adults. Children learn about feelings—what they are and what to do with them—from their parents and other important adults in their lives. Unfortunately, sometimes what they learn doesn't help them much.

What Are Feelings, Anyway?

Christians sometimes think that they shouldn't have feelings (except for the "good" ones, of course) and become disappointed and disillusioned when disrespect, anger, and strife invade their families. Yet the Bible contains Scriptures about guilt, loneliness, fear, envy, anger, and hatred, as well as joy, peace, and love. Even Jesus felt anger, throwing the money changers out of the Temple and cursing the poor fig tree; apparently, the Lord knew we would have a multitude of feelings (some of them highly uncomfortable) and intended us to learn to manage them wisely.

Psalm 139:14 sums up how we feel about one of God's most complex and excellent creations: the human brain. "I will give thanks to You; for I am fearfully and wonderfully made. Wonderful are your works. And my soul knows it very well." Current research seems to indicate that emotions are generated primarily by parts of the human brain called the amygdala and the hippocampus, and are intended simply to provide information. Not only that: there is a "neural net" of brain cells around the heart, and another in the belly. The phrases "my heart told me" or "gut instinct" turn out to be almost literally true! In fact, without emotions it is difficult to make decisions, weigh options, or enjoy life. Feelings are neither good nor bad; everyone has them, and feelings by themselves don't cause problems. Each of us—adult and child—is entitled to whatever feelings we have. However, what you *do* with your feelings may be hurtful or inappropriate. Consider the following examples:

- Kristen is 16 years old. Her father has allowed her to drive the family car on her first Friday night outing with friends. Kristen doesn't have much experience in crowded parking lots and backs into a light pole at the movie theater. She is *worried* and *afraid*. Her father will be *angry* and *disappointed*, may not let her drive the car again, and may insist that Kristen pay for the damage. Kristen tells her father that someone must have backed into the car; she doesn't know how that dent got there.

- Pamela has had a rough day. She has three-year-old triplets, Courtney, Callie and Caitlin, all of whom have special needs because of their premature birth. Two of the girls were awake most of the night with ear infections, and Pamela is exhausted. She has several doctors' and therapy appointments scheduled for the day, and the triplets are *cranky* and *irritable*. By lunchtime, Pamela is *frustrated* and *annoyed*; she also feels *guilty* because she isn't as patient with the girls as she normally is. When Courtney refuses to get into her car seat after a long afternoon of appointments, Pamela's nerves snap. "Don't be such a brat!" she says angrily, and slaps Courtney's cheek.

- Jeremy is nine years old. His friends at school all own a popular new toy, but Jeremy's parents don't like the toy and will not give him permission to buy it. Jeremy feels *embarrassed, angry,* and *jealous*. One afternoon, Jeremy goes with his best friend's family to the local toy store. When no one is looking, he slips the toy into the pocket of his jacket. Later, when his parents ask him where he got it, he tells them he found it.

The emotions Kristen, Pamela, and Jeremy felt were perfectly understandable. The actions they chose, however, were dishonest, hurtful, or inappropriate. Part of becoming a mature person is recognizing that what you *feel* can (and often should) be different than what you *do*. For both adults and children, however, this process takes both patience and practice.

It isn't always necessary to "do" something with feelings. In fact, one reason people often "stuff" or squelch their emotions is because they fear that those emotions will somehow take over and cause them to behave badly. And, as we mentioned before, Christians sometimes believe that having "negative" feelings indicates a lack of faith or spiritual weakness. Everyone, however, has feelings. In addition, emotions that aren't dealt with in a healthy manner don't just go away. They sometimes fester and ooze all over a person's life, scabbing up like a painful cut or scrape, thereby putting a 'lid' on living life to the fullest. Or they might leak out (in the form of resentment or depression), or explode in rage or frustration. Learning to recognize and manage feelings is an important task for adults and children alike. (See the *Positive Discipline Feeling Faces Chart* in this chapter and identify the feeling that best describes what you are feeling right now!)

> *Part of becoming a mature person is recognizing that what you feel can (and often should) be different than what you do.*

Positive Discipline
Feeling Faces

Illustrations by Paula Gray
www.positivediscipline.com

Understanding the Message of Nonverbal Communication

Dan is in his study working at the computer when twelve-year-old Matthew bursts in the front door. Matthew's chin is trembling; he slams the door roughly, rattling the pictures on the wall, and stomps off to his bedroom. That door slams, too.

Not a word has been spoken, but Dan understands instantly that his son is terribly upset. Matthew has sent a powerful nonverbal message to his father. Adults usually rely on words to communicate. (In fact, we use lots and lots of them and then wonder why our children so often tune us out.) But sometimes the most powerful messages we send to each other use no words at all. We send them with our facial expressions, our tone of voice, our posture, the eye contact we make (or refuse to make), and the "energy" of our feelings.

If you doubt that feelings exude energy, think about a time you walked into a room where people had been arguing. You could probably feel the static and tension in the air, even if no one was speaking. In fact, all of us have the ability to perceive emotional energy and nonverbal communication by using our system of mirror neurons, which allow humans to perceive and duplicate the movements and emotions of other humans. In fact, experts estimate that we communicate as much as eighty percent of our messages to each other in these nonverbal ways. Words may lie, but energy and nonverbal messages rarely do. A resource to check is Dan J. Siegel and Mary Hartzell's book, *Parenting From the Inside Out,* Tarcher, 2003. In this book and other works by Siegel, they help explain how interpersonal relationships impact the development of the brain.

Young children in particular rely heavily on "reading" and sending nonverbal messages because their ability to use language doesn't develop fully until they are several years old. Unfortunately, parents sometimes send mixed messages: "No, I'm not mad," they say, while scrunching up their eyebrows and clenching their fists. Children will instinctively trust the nonverbal message more than the verbal one. And as we've seen with Dan and Matthew, parents can learn to read the nonverbal messages their children send, too.

Pay careful attention the next time you have a conversation with someone you love. Do you make eye contact with that person? Do they look back at you? Some communications researchers have noted that parents tend to make eye contact with their children when they are angry, and to avoid direct eye contact at other times. What is your facial expression saying? Your tone of voice? What about your posture and body position? Do your nonverbal messages match the words you are saying, or are you sending a mixed message?

If you're still wondering why this is important, consider the message "I love you." Most of us say this casually, almost carelessly, assuming that the words themselves are enough to get the message across. But are they? The next time you want a child to truly *hear* this message, get down on her level and look directly into her eyes. Smile, and use a warm tone of voice. You may even want to put an arm around her shoulders. Now say, "I love you." Can you feel a hug coming? Even when you are angry, your message will get through if your love gets through first. You might say, "Honey, I love you so much and nothing can change that. And I felt very angry when you hit your brother. When you and I both calm down, I have faith that we can figure out a way to help your brother feel better and to solve the problem in respectful ways."

Sometimes, too, nonverbal communication makes even the most eloquent words unnecessary. Martha is fourteen years old. She loves to sing, and worked hard to prepare for honor choir auditions. Her two best friends were both selected, but Martha was not. Now she is curled forlornly on the sofa with her knees under her chin, doing some reading for her English class at school. She looks as sad and discouraged as she must feel. Martha's mother is a wise woman and knows that words may not be the best way to help her daughter right now. So, as she walks by the sofa, she reaches out and gives Martha a sympathetic smile and a gentle hug around the shoulders. Martha smiles wanly in response. Martha's mother knows she cannot "fix" or erase her daughter's disappointment, but she has let Martha know that she loves and empathizes with her. For now, that is enough.

The Power of Active Listening

The truth is that with the best of intentions, parents often want to "fix" or change their children's emotions. "Cheer up," we tell them. "There's nothing to be afraid of," we say firmly, or "Don't you be angry with me, young man!" But feelings are not so easily changed, as you will recognize if anyone has ever tried to tell *you* how to feel. Wise parents are aware that children's behavior is shaped by what they think, feel, and decide about themselves. There is an old saying that "what most people need is a good listening to." And careful attention to emotions—a skill we will call "active listening"—is one of the best ways to help children manage their feelings, feel understood, and move on to solving problems.

Active listening allows parents to demonstrate compassion, something the Bible encourages us to show for one another. "Live in harmony with one another, be sympathetic, love as brothers, be compassionate and humble. Do not repay evil with evil or insult with insult, but with blessing, because to this you were called so that you may inherit a blessing." (1 Peter 3:8-9) Compassion and tenderheartedness (rather than judgment, criticism, lecturing, and nagging) are ways we both share and receive blessing. And compassion without judgment is one of the best ways to create a sense of belonging and significance for children.

Remember Dan and Matthew? Dan had been working in his study when Matthew slammed his way into the house and disappeared into his room. Being a perfectly normal father, Dan's first reaction was annoyance. "That kid!" he thought. "How many times have I told him not to slam the door? I've had it with his rudeness!"

Dan saved his computer file and started down the hall towards his son's room. But as he approached the closed door, he slowed to a walk, and finally stood still.

Dan took a deep breath, remembering suddenly what it was like to be twelve years old. "Lord," he breathed quietly, "help me to reach out to my son." Then Dan remembered a lesson from the parenting class his church had offered a couple of months earlier. What did they say to do in moments like this? Oh yes—feelings. Perhaps that would be a good place to begin.

Dan knocked softly on Matthew's door. "Hey, Matt," he said.

"What do you want?" came the gruff reply from inside. Again Dan stifled his impatience. "I just wanted to make sure you were okay, son," he said. "You looked so hurt and angry when you came in."

There was a long silence; then the door opened slowly and Dan saw his son's tear-streaked face. Something made Dan remain silent. Instead of speaking, he simply reached an arm towards his son and Matthew moved into his embrace. After a long, silent hug, Matthew stepped away, struggling visibly to control his emotions.

"You look so sad, Matt," Dan said quietly. "What's going on?"

> *...careful attention to emotions—a skill we will call "active listening"—is one of the best ways to help children manage their feelings, feel understood, and move on to solving problems.*

Matthew took a deep breath. "Luke's dad has cancer," he said softly. Dan was stunned; Luke and Matthew had been best friends since preschool. They went to school and church together, played Little League and soccer together, and spent hours just hanging out. The boys were constantly in and out of each other's homes, and Luke's dad had always been a second father to Matthew.

Dan felt relief that he hadn't begun this conversation by scolding Matthew for slamming the door. As he looked into his son's face, he suddenly saw the confusion, fear, and sorrow there. Dan drew his son down onto the bed beside him, and suggested that they say a prayer for Luke, his father, and his family. When they had finished, Matthew looked up into his father's face.

"If this can happen to Luke and his dad," he said softly, "how do I know it won't happen to you? This is *so* unfair, Dad. Mr. Martin is a good man and he loves his kids so much. Why does God let stuff like this happen?"

"I don't know, Matt. It's pretty confusing, isn't it?" Dan was wise enough to know that these questions wouldn't be resolved in a single conversation. He also didn't try to make Matthew "feel better," instead giving him time and permission to absorb the real pain he was experiencing. Dan chose to focus on his son's feelings, reflecting back his anguish and fear. And by focusing on Matthew's emotions rather than just his behavior, Dan gave his son a way to express what was *really* going on for him, and built a foundation that would enable father and son to help each other through the challenging times ahead. Dan also learned the wisdom of Proverbs 15:1: "A gentle answer turns away wrath, but a harsh word stirs up anger."

> Children who feel understood and whose emotions have been validated are almost always more willing to work on solving problems and correcting behavior.

Notice that active listening does not mean you condone poor behavior. Had it been important, Dan could have found a moment later on to speak with Matthew about slamming the doors. Nor does active listening mean that you agree with your child's feelings. It simply provides a bridge of understanding and empathy so that the people you love can feel heard, and can move on to problem solving and cooperation.

In their book, *Raising Cain: Protecting the Emotional Life of Boys,* (Ballantine Books; 2000), Dan Kindlon and Michael Thompson speak of the need to give our children "emotional literacy," the ability to be aware of, to accept, and to manage their feelings. Active listening—simply labeling the emotion you believe your child is feeling and reflecting it back to him—helps him learn to identify his own emotions and also teaches him that what he *feels* is always acceptable, even when what he *does* may not be. It also opens the door for families to share difficult experiences and feelings in an atmosphere of respect and love, rather than withdrawing into silence or avoiding the painful emotions that are an inevitable part of life for all of us.

Don't simply assume that you know how your child feels: be willing to check, and to truly listen. As difficult as it can sometimes be, don't take your children's emotions personally. Instead, ask questions that show genuine curiosity, and be willing to "listen with your lips together" to the answers you receive. There is almost always a hidden message underneath the spoken message. The words "I hate you" could really mean in feeling language, "I feel hurt that you don't seem to have time for me, or favor Billy over me, or make me feel conditionally loved when you focus so much on my grades." Children who feel understood and whose emotions have been validated are almost always more willing to work on solving problems and correcting behavior.

You can practice active listening with happy feelings, too. "Boy, you sure look cheerful today!" may be just the invitation your child is waiting for to share her most wonderful experiences. You can help your children learn to recognize and verbalize their feelings as well as yourself by using the Feeling Faces Chart. Look at the chart in this chapter with your child and ask, "Can you find a face that comes close to expressing how you feel right now?"

Using Positive Time Out to Manage Emotions

You may remember positive time-out from Chapter 8 about parenting tools. Positive time-out is an excellent discipline tool, but it is especially effective in helping everyone in your family remain respectful and cooperative even in the face of strong emotions.

If you have young children, you have undoubtedly witnessed the atmospheric disturbance known as a temper tantrum. (Many parents have thrown a few tantrums of their own, often in response to their children's!) Feeling angry, provoked, or resentful rarely brings out the best in anyone. It can be quite effective to combine active listening with a positive time-out. For instance, when your child becomes defiant or angry, you may say, "I can see how frustrated you are right now. Why don't you go to your cool-off spot until you feel better? When you have calmed down, come find me and we'll work together on a way to solve this problem." Another possibility is to say, "Would you like to go to your cool-off spot alone, or would you like me to go with you?" This emphasizes that a cool-off spot is not punishment. If your child does invite you to go, don't talk unless she starts the conversation. Just sit quietly offering love and support.

Often it is the parent who truly needs a moment to calm down, to think rationally, and to act with respect and dignity. You can tell your child, "I am feeling really angry right now and don't want to say or do something I will regret. I am going to take a moment to cool off; I'll meet you back here in five minutes and we'll talk about what just happened."

Notice that this is not the punitive time-out that so many parents rely on. ("Stop that before I count to three, or you're in time-out!") Allowing everyone time to calm down is not permissiveness; it is often the most effective way to change behavior and invite cooperation, and to avoid the yelling, commanding, and arguing that can become so destructive. Can you think of a better way to teach children to manage their feelings than by taking some time for rational thought to return before they decide what to do?

"Well, What About My Feelings?"

Children almost always know more about what you think and feel than you suppose. Remember, they are unusually perceptive at reading emotional "energy" and body language.

And because children are egocentric for much of their early years—that is, they tend to believe that other people's actions and feelings happen because of *them*—it can be quite helpful when you simply talk to your children about your own emotions (without blaming them, of course).

Here are some examples of appropriate emotional honesty:

- "I'm feeling frustrated because I have an important meeting at work this morning and we're running late. I'd appreciate your help in getting your school things together."
- "I'm feeling angry at your father right now. We're taking a time-out, and we'll talk a little later."
- "When you don't come home on time, I feel worried that something might have happened to you. I'd appreciate it if you could give me a call when you're going to be late."

Stick to the facts, be accurate about your feelings, and, if appropriate, explain why you feel as you do and what you'd like to see happen. If that seems impossible, it may be a good idea to take a time-out before you say anything at all!

Adults often squelch their feelings, or say one thing when it's obvious they feel something else. Two points are important to the effective expression of emotional honesty. The first is to know that it is okay for you to feel what you feel, think what you think, and want what you want. The second is that no matter how respectfully you express yourself, others may not feel or think the same way, and are not obligated to give you what you want just because you asked. Still, respectful honesty is always more effective than manipulation, withdrawal, anger, or expecting someone else to read your mind. ("If you really loved me, you would know that.") Remember, *mutual* respect is the key to successful relationships.

Growing a Listening Heart

Parenting isn't easy, especially when parents must deal with the stresses and challenges of a busy world as well as the needs and behavior of their growing children. Many families enter counseling asking for help in "communication" but it's rarely because they have trouble talking—in fact, sometimes everyone in the family is talking at once! Communication is really about *listening*—to words, to feelings, and to actions—and real listening begins in the heart.

You will not always like everything your child (or your partner) has to say. But when you can practice active listening, remain calm and respectful, and speak your own heart with kindness and firmness, communication is rarely a problem and everyone in your family will feel a sense of belonging and significance. What's more, the Lord then has the opportunity to grow in us the fruit of His spirit, which is "love, joy, peace, patience, kindness, goodness, faithfulness, gentleness and self-control. Against such things there is no law." (Galatians 5:22-23) These are feelings all of us, parents and children alike, welcome into our homes and hearts.

Chapter 11

Family Meetings

"Let us not give up meeting together, as some are in the habit of doing, but let us encourage one another ..."

(Hebrews 10:25)

> "Time for our family meeting, everyone," Marjorie hollers to the far corners of her home. She's looking forward to getting everyone together again. "Finally, after six weeks of family meetings, it seems so good—so natural," Marjorie thinks to herself on her way to the kitchen "round-table." Dad is already at the sink washing his hands. Sierra, age twelve, is excited because she has prepared everyone's favorite dessert. Mark and Melanie, both eight years old, come in the back door. They grumble all the way into the kitchen about having to do this "right in the middle of our scooter race." Then, out of nowhere, Mark hurls a bombshell, "Oh great—another 'Mom's meeting.' I wonder what great chores I get to volunteer for this week." Marjorie's happy smile quickly dissolves as she thinks, "Mom's meeting? Where did Mark get that idea anyway?" Quickly remembering that other families have worked through these obstacles, Marjorie remarks, "Mark, I'm putting your concern on the family agenda so we can all talk about it and get it resolved."

The Family Meeting

One of the most powerful family rituals to help create a sense of belonging in the family, as well to teach the characteristics and life skills that we have explored throughout this book, is the family meeting. Like class meetings, which serve as the foundation for the Positive Discipline program in schools, family meetings provide an effective means of teaching a multitude of skills within an atmosphere of respect and appreciation.

We often hear about families holding family meetings only in response to a problem or challenge that is facing them. One woman, who recently went back to work as a teacher after her three children were all in school, told us that she held a family meeting about a month before her first day at work to parcel out the many chores that she had previously done herself. As much as we applaud her decision to hold a family meeting for this purpose, it might have been unnecessary if she had been holding them regularly throughout the years. Those chores might have already been spoken for, amid a growing family atmosphere of cooperation and teamwork. And family meeting time might be eagerly anticipated as something more than "Mom's meeting," as in the story above.

As we discuss family meetings, it is important to remember that perfection is not the goal. You can work instead to create an atmosphere of mutual respect, cooperation, and fun. You won't get discouraged when you realize that all of the mistakes, complaints, successes, and failures add to the learning process. Some of our children who complained when we had family meetings now have organized dorm meetings, roommate meetings, and family meetings in their own families. And many meetings are very enjoyable. We enjoy reading some of our old family meeting notebooks as much as we enjoy looking at old photographs.

Now, we don't want to imply that the sole purpose of family meetings is to spread the task of chores throughout the family (though that is often a pleasant result). Family meetings do so much more, as we'll discover in this chapter. But first, let's go over the mechanics of the family meeting.

Simply stated, the family meeting is a weekly opportunity for all family members to give and receive compliments, share interests and concerns, discuss family issues, and plan for family fun. It is best that nothing be allowed to interrupt the family meeting—let the answering machine pick up the telephone messages, and by all means shut off the media. (Yes, even your smart phones and electronic tablets—whatever communication or entertainment system you or your children are currently enjoying!) This shows respect for the time each person is giving to the family meeting. When family meetings are interrupted, family communication is disrupted, and family members wonder why they ever came to the table.

A simple agenda for the family meeting is suggested here:

- Prayer, scriptural reading, Bible story, or other inspirational story. You can invite each family member to take turns leading this opening moment.
- Compliments, appreciations, and/or sharing of something positive that happened during the week. (The revised original *Positive Discipline* by Jane Nelsen calls this a "time for gratitude.")
- Agenda items such as those listed here for sharing, discussion, or problem solving:
  - Calendar
  - Chores
  - Allowances
  - Additional Announcements
  - Celebration or fun family activity

Prayer and/or Scriptural Reading

"For where two or more come together in my name, there am I with them." (Matthew 18:20) We can think of no better way to start a family meeting than with a prayer. Welcoming Jesus into the process and asking His blessing on what the family is doing is a powerful way to keep the family focused on supporting each other and working through the many issues that face today's families with respect, dignity, and grace. Calling upon God's presence also follows the model Jesus gave us as He worked with his spiritual family—his disciples. Jesus called his disciples together to experience a gathering and strengthening time of fellowship before sending them out into the world to lead their own daily lives, often scattered far apart from the presence of other disciples.

We also recommend that the opportunity to lead the family in prayer or to read from the Scriptures be shared on a rotating basis. A child's Bible, a child's book of prayers, and selected memory verses can help younger children contribute meaningfully when it is their turn. Your family may prefer to start the meeting with prayer to invite Jesus to your table and save a special reading or memory verse for the meeting's closure after the time of celebration.

> *...perfection is not the goal. You can work instead to create an atmosphere of mutual respect, cooperation, and fun.*

Some families we know use the closure part of their family meeting time to discuss how to respond to the message of that week's sermon at church and put God's word into action throughout the week. We also know families who do their memorization work based on the sermon shared at church. At some family meetings, family members might discuss a way they have been touched spiritually in the past week. When asked to lead the family in a devotion or prayer from their heart, even very young children are often profound.

By varying the format of the spiritual portion of the family meeting while keeping the item as a regular part of your family meeting agenda, you and your children can look forward to the growth and inspiration you will share. You will also begin a tradition that will nourish your family throughout your lives together.

Compliments and Appreciations

One of the most humbling experiences we have when leading Positive Discipline workshops is seeing adults sitting in a circle, taking turns exchanging compliments during a practice family meeting. Rarely does this happen without at least a few tears of appreciation being shed. Kind words are all too rare in these hectic and stressful times. The giving and receiving of compliments is an underused skill in our culture, let alone within the walls of the family home. Think about how you responded the last time you were given a compliment. Was it along the lines of: "Oh, it was nothing." "No big deal." "It's just an old dress." Or was your response just an embarrassed silence? Should we not, instead, respond with "thank you" or "I appreciate that" or "thanks for noticing" when given a compliment? The truth is that most of us are reluctant compliment receivers, and we're not too good at giving them, either. Perhaps we fear that we will embarrass the recipient or believe that a positive comment isn't important. We may even believe that a compliment or appreciation is dangerous.

Many Christians have been taught that "pride goeth before a fall" and fear that offering compliments or appreciation to their children will create a dangerous sense of pride and boastfulness. Actually, the Bible says, "Let another praise you, and not your own mouth; someone else, and not your own lips." (Proverbs 27:2) There is a difference between offering appreciation or a well-deserved encouragement and boasting of one's own accomplishments. Children can be thanked for their contributions and taught to value their own worth and abilities, and still taught that humility before others and God is a valuable attribute.

> *When family members first take time to create a mutually respectful sense of appreciation and cooperation at the family meeting table, it is easier to work together on problems.*

Family meetings provide an excellent opportunity, in a formal, yet non-threatening atmosphere, to practice the skills of giving and receiving compliments. A compliment can be as simple as, "I would like to compliment (or appreciate, or thank) _____ for _____." An example might be: "I would like to compliment Dad for fixing the flat tire on my bicycle." Or, "I would like to thank Melanie for helping me with the dishes even though it wasn't her chore this week." Or even (from Dad to Mom): "I want to tell Mom how much I appreciated her taking care of the plumbing problem in the kitchen instead of leaving it for me to do when I got home." In each case, the response is the simple two-word phrase: "Thank you."

Compliments are important because they help provide an atmosphere of support and openness within which discussion can occur about issues where there may be disagreement. When family members first take time to create a mutually respectful sense of appreciation and cooperation at the family meeting table, it is easier to work together on problems. As we have said before, all of us (parents and children alike) do better when we feel better, and problem solving and cooperation are easier when everyone in the family feels appreciated and welcomed.

It takes time for the skill of complimenting to become a habit, especially for children who are far more comfortable complaining about each other than complimenting each other. (Actually, research on human behavior shows that a minimum of twenty-one days is needed to turn any skill into a habit. That would be at least three weekly meetings with eighteen days of practice sandwiched in!) So don't become discouraged. The more practice we get in "catching people doing good" the easier "good-finding" becomes.

Share Something Positive

As an alternative (or in addition) to offering compliments (especially when family members are first learning the art of the compliment circle), each member of your family may enjoy sharing one positive thing that has happened to them during the past week. Marjorie, our example at the beginning of this chapter, found that not only had she used family meetings only to resolve chore issues, but she and her husband had let the "good-finding" slip—at the request of their children, who were not particularly comfortable giving—or taking—compliments.

Giving compliments or sharing positive experiences helps to set a positive and friendly atmosphere for the other topics on the family agenda, particularly when family members may have been arguing about something the entire week. An example of a positive sharing sounds like this: "Something positive that happened to me was that I found salmon on sale at the grocery store for our supper tonight."

One of the authors gave a "home-fun" activity assignment to families in her church who were attending a workshop on improving family communication. The objective was simple: 'just get people to the table and have them *want* to be there.' (Ultimately, of course, the goal was to help families hold regular family meetings together.) The activity was this: "Ask each family member to bring one object that has special meaning to him or her to the family table. Spend at least twenty minutes listening to each other's stories and discussing each other's objects."

A few weeks later, one of the parents shared the results of this activity. Her daughter had brought a necklace to the table that had been Mom's when she was little. Mariah had been given the necklace some years back and both of them had forgotten about it. Mariah had brought that object to the table to tell her Mom how special this memory was, and that she appreciated her Mom's generosity in sharing this and many other pieces of jewelry through the years. Mariah said she even remembered seeing a picture of her Mom wearing the necklace when she was little, so they began a review of family scrapbooks that continued through the weeks to come. Maria and her daughter had been experiencing some typical tension through the teen years and both of them were grateful for this moment of love and connection.

Agenda Items for Sharing, Discussion, or Problem-solving

Agenda items can be problems that need solutions. But sometimes they can just be opportunities to share feelings while others listen or opportunities to discuss concerns without the need to fix things. The goal is to meet each week regardless of how full or scant the agenda is. A family meeting whose only agenda is to share prayer, appreciations, and a time of celebration is just as important as a family meeting where every part of our suggested agenda needs attention.

Many families provide an agenda so each family member can write down items for discussion in advance. (Yes, Mom and Dad are part of this agenda-making—but not the *only* contributors!) Anyone in the family can write down the issue he or she wishes to discuss and then, at the family meeting, each issue is addressed in sequence. Young children can draw a picture or use their favorite color marker to indicate that they have something to contribute. Sometimes it isn't possible to discuss each item on the agenda, so it may be necessary to prioritize the items, saving items not discussed for the next weekly family meeting.

This agenda can take any form your family creates. It could be a sheet of paper posted on the refrigerator, a computer-generated form, a shoe box with a slot cut in the top, or any other convenient means to allow for the writing down of items of concern. Some families we know create a kind of "yearly family meeting journal," which is kept in plain sight on the kitchen counter. In this journal are recorded the agenda, minutes, decisions, and comments of each family meeting, along with a snapshot or two of the special family fun times which may follow the meetings. (This kind of record is fun as the children grow and can look back to their earlier writing and concerns.) Other families simply give each member a chance to speak, without a formal agenda or recorded minutes. In any case, each family member who wishes to do so needs to be given time to contribute.

> No matter what form calendar-time takes for your family, it can rescue everyone from relying on memory for important occasions, nipping confusion, stress, and hurt feelings in the bud.

How does the meeting proceed? The first agenda item is read and the family member who placed it on the agenda is asked if this is still a concern. (If no formal agenda has been written down, each family member takes turns bringing up ideas and issues to list on the agenda before the meeting begins, while the note-taker writes down the items.) If the item is no longer a concern, the next agenda item is chosen. Interestingly, many items placed on the agenda during the week turn out not to be a problem come family meeting day. The very act of writing the problem down often serves as a way to vent feelings, and that may be all that is needed. Sometimes the people with the problem solve it before the meeting—without the family's help. These situations often become encouragement opportunities, especially when they involve a sibling fight. Also, some time will have passed. And while time doesn't heal all wounds, it certainly does heal some of them.

If the agenda item is still a problem, the family member who has raised the issue is asked what solution she thinks might best solve it. Then other family members are invited to offer their comments and ideas for solutions. "Brainstorming" is a particularly effective way to get ideas on the table at this point. Brainstorming means writing down all possible suggestions— even the funny or impossible ones—without comment or criticism at that moment. There are several reasons for doing this: Children who offer a solution that is promptly shot down usually become unwilling to speak up later on. And even an unworkable solution may trigger a good idea for someone else. Write down all the suggestions on a big piece of paper; then you can evaluate and discuss them together.

It is usually better to choose solutions by consensus, rather than by a vote. (Remember, voting creates "winners and losers," and losers often feel no inclination to participate in a decision they didn't share.) Then the next item is addressed. If the agenda item only affects the person who put the item on the agenda, that person should be allowed to make any decisions about a solution (hopefully after careful consideration of the helpful comments from other family members). You can take time at future meetings to explore how well the solution worked and what happened.

Calendar

These days, scheduling can be a nightmare for even the smallest of families. With many homes having two working parents and active youngsters, it is extremely helpful to share and record activities during calendar-time. This allows all family members to plan their time wisely, and to know in advance when their presence will be needed. Some families decide to make an agreement that "if it's not on the calendar, the family is not obligated to honor the activity." Occasional lapses in memory are tolerated, because no one is perfect. (Even parents are sometimes grateful for forgiveness!)

Some families have wipe-off calendars, while some print out computer forms. Others have individual calendars or technological devices that are brought to the meetings to be updated simultaneously with the family calendar. Many schools have school calendars for their students pre-printed with all school activities for the year. No matter what form calendar-time takes for your family, it can rescue everyone from relying on memory for important occasions, nipping confusion, stress, and hurt feelings in the bud.

Chores

While family meetings probably won't be popular and successful in your home if they are *only* about chores, family meetings certainly are an effective way to deal with the inevitable chore disputes that arise. We believe that chores are actually "family work," tasks that help the family function more smoothly and thus are the responsibility of every member of the family. (See the book *Chores Without Wars,* Lott and Intner, Taylor Trade Publishing, 2005, for additional and practical help.)

The authors have plenty of chore stories to share. A colleague who has been working with families for years helping them learn to implement family meetings shared with us how the meetings got started in his household. His wife, who had recently gone back to work as a teacher, felt that she was being expected to take on too much of the responsibility for the household chores. So she called a family meeting during which she presented a list of all the chores that needed to be done to keep the family running, making it clear that from now on the chores were to be shared. Dad, Mom, and their two children discussed the options available, came to an agreement through consensus, and set the plan in motion. From then on, family meetings became a regular feature of their weekly activities. (Dad, who ended up with the responsibility for cooking dinners, informed us that he has since developed a fondness for take-out pizza.)

Another chore story comes from the Hughes'household. Their first computer came in helpful about the same time they started having family meetings, and Dad created a master-list of all the chores to be done in one week (including all the parents' jobs that kids couldn't do yet, such as driving the soccer car-pool). They all signed up for the chores on a first-come, first-serve basis. These chore sign-up negotiations consumed much of their first family meetings, as each of the three children attempted to get the "easiest" jobs. Eventually, a pattern emerged and the chores found their regular doers.

One week, when Eric's regular self-appointed job of scooping out the cat litter was taken before he could sign up for it, he reluctantly agreed to do one of Wendy's regular jobs: helping the designated cook-of-the-day. He discovered that he enjoyed the variety and challenge of this new skill. Unlike the Dad in the previous story who discovered the benefits of take-out pizza, Eric's experience with cooking eventually produced an adult chef of some distinction. And surprisingly, Eric attributes this skill to his early cooking days. (You may never know the positive impact of chore sign-ups until much later.)

Lucy was a single mom for almost nine years. She admits that she made an effort to "help" her son choose dusting as his chore, mostly because her own mother had assigned this task to her and Lucy hated to dust. However, her son cooperated only grudgingly; he dusted only on the edges of things and frequently "forgot." When Lucy was willing to be more respectful, she earned more cooperation: her son volunteered at a family meeting that he didn't mind vacuuming, but hated dusting. Lucy decided that getting willing help was far better than arguing and nagging, sighed, and did her own dusting while her son happily vacuumed.

In the Nelsen family, chores were rotated once a week. The kids came up with many plans for rotation. Sometimes they chose their chores for the week from a jar. Other times they had fun "spinning" for their chores. (The children had helped Mom make a chore spinner from a paper plate with pictures of chores on the outside of the plate and a spinner in the middle.)

The reason they had many different plans is because enthusiasm for chores would last only a week or two, even when the kids were respectfully involved in choosing their chores. One of the better plans was to put all the chores on a white board; children who got there first chose the chore they would do. Mom was excited about this idea because she could quit trying to rotate and be fair. For the first week, the children set their alarm clocks trying to get the "best" chores first. However, they soon decided it wasn't worth that much effort, but willingly did whatever chores were left when they got around to it.

Remember that no matter what the chores and tasks in your family are, it is important to have realistic expectations and to make sure you "take time for training." Be sure your children know *how* tasks should be done and feel comfortable doing them—it will save lots of time spent complaining, debating, and whining, and free up your family meeting agenda for more enjoyable items.

> ...no matter what the chores and tasks in your family are, it is important to have realistic expectations and to make sure you "take time for training."

However you choose to accomplish the task of getting family cooperation for chores, it is important for just that reason—family cooperation. This is why we don't believe it is a good idea to pay children for doing their chores.

Allowances

Many parents in our parenting workshops ask about allowances. We believe it is wise to avoid putting the words *chores* and *allowances* in the same sentence. They are separate issues in families where value lies not in what you do, but rather in who you are. Allowances, we believe, are not the product of doing chores or not doing them. An allowance is given to meet expenses and to teach the value of money, while chores teach responsibility, give and take, and family cooperation.

It is a good idea to teach financial skills within the family, including how to maintain a checking and saving account system, how to budget, how to earn money, and how to give back to the Lord a portion of what He has given us. An easy way to teach these concepts is by teaching the "3 $'s" about money as early as possible in a child's life: money allows us to $pend, to $ave, and to $erve. Each person in your family has expenses, items to spend money on. Some are expected, while others are considered entertainment expenses. (It is important to teach children the difference between "wants" and "needs.") For children, this may include school lunches, movie or skating admission fees, and some clothing items, perhaps those beyond what is budgeted for in the family's finances.

Some families have a list of extra jobs "for hire." This list includes the job (such as washing the car or organizing a closet) with the amount that will be paid. When children need extra money, they can choose some of these jobs instead of begging for handouts. As children grow, earning money through babysitting, cutting the neighbors' lawns, or managing paper routes can become a very important way to gain additional income above and beyond a family allowance. Many items are too costly to purchase all at once and require children to develop the habit of saving. For children these items may include vacation money, a bicycle, a scooter, CD's, a DVD player, a computer, a car, or to help fund a college education.

The last $, $ervice, means that a part of a child's allowance is put in the offering at church (rather than putting the parents' change in the plate), sent to a designated service organization, or used to purchase an item for a needy family in the neighborhood.

The percentages of each $ can be determined within the family. The Bible teaches the law of tithing; if ten percent is the amount your family agrees is best, then this is a concept you will want to teach by example. It is by observing a spirit of giving within their family that children grow up to be cheerful givers themselves. A paraphrased Scripture reference is 2 Corinthians 9:7: "We are to give what we have decided in our hearts, not reluctantly, or because we "have to" under the law, but because we want to, and want to do so cheerfully."

Discovering a way to discuss money matters that makes sense to your family is an important part of family meetings. Whether or not all family finances are discussed at this meeting is up to you as the parent. Financial up-dates and discussions about family finances can help children learn about financial planning. This area is a parental responsibility, however, and many parents choose not to discuss issues that may worry children, particularly in times of family distress. If family finances are tight enough to impact family vacation planning or activity choices for the children (such as someone wanting to take piano *and* guitar lessons), the situation can be discussed as a family and a plan for dealing with the final decision left to the parents.

Additional Announcements

This part of a family meeting is reserved for something special a family member has to say. Perhaps it is report card time, maybe Mom has a work opportunity to discuss with the family, or Dad may have a business trip coming up that he would like to add some family time to. It could be that college acceptance time is here, or someone got a raise at work or won the lottery (just kidding).

> *...special family time is a planned application of family "super-glue."*

Announcements are items that may not require discussion or problem-solving now though they may be items to think about in preparation for the next meeting. They are quick items on the agenda, a sort of "FYI" (for your information) topic.

You may find that announcement time occasionally runs into celebration time, especially when a family member has good news. Today, many mail-order catalogs show various versions of a family "celebration plate" that is put at a person's place who has a birthday or other event to celebrate. It might be fun to put this designated plate before the person who has a special announcement and have the family wondering through the meeting what good news will end the family's time together.

Celebration

We recommend ending each family meeting with a dessert, a game or story time, or some other fun activity. Here is where a family Scripture, a prayer, or an inspirational poem could be shared, rather than as the first item of business in the family meeting. Maybe this is a piece of Scripture that a family member chooses for each person to work on memorizing through the week in preparation for the next meeting. Everyone in the family over the age of three (the younger the child, the bigger and fuller the feeling of pride over what they have planned) can take turns in organizing this time of celebration. Occasionally there may only be time at the end of the family meeting for a short dessert, story, or game. When this happens, the family can plan a family time or meal during the coming week that everyone honors. Regardless of what happens, special family time is a planned application of family "super-glue." Without it, we may grow up in families we never really know. Without it, we may never value our family members as the unique treasure they are meant to be.

Why all this structure and formality, you may be asking? In another time, in another place, we probably would have no need for formal, structured family meetings. But today, family members seem to be racing off in all different directions, rarely sitting down together to talk. Television and technology create barriers to focused dialogue in many families. Stresses and pressures unknown a generation ago require that families learn to compensate in an organized way for the culture in which we live. Somehow we need to ensure that at least once a week all family members will be listened to and affirmed.

Remember, too, that family meetings teach children many important life skills. They learn to look for positive things to verbalize about each other. They learn how to brainstorm for solutions—and the importance of looking for solutions instead of blame. And they learn tolerance and appreciation for differences (and what family doesn't have several different personality styles?) They learn excellent communication skills, both speaking and listening.

Many families use a "talking stick" during their family meetings. Only the person holding the talking stick can speak, an effective way to help young children learn to take turns. The Talking Stick originates from Native American tribes in the Great Plains region. It is simply a stick, maybe a foot-and-a-half to two feet long, decorated as desired with feathers, strips of leather, and beads, and held by the person whose turn it is to talk. Your family's talking stick could be created together as a family project.

Perhaps your family has a shell from a shell collection gathered on family vacations, or some other valued family object that could be used in place of a talking stick. It is wise to remember (and to teach your children) that speaking requires listening, and that they must listen to the person who holds the talking stick as carefully as they would want to be listened to.

Concerns to Consider

These thoughts may help you begin effective, respectful meetings in your family:

- A participant in one of our parenting seminars observed: "We had family meetings when I was a kid. We all sat together around the dinner table with Dad at the head telling us what we were going to do, how we were going to do it, and when we were going to do it." (Ah, "Dad's Meetings!") Clearly, that's not what we have in mind here. The purpose of the family meeting is to provide a time when each family member can be listened to, have their ideas thoughtfully considered, and be affirmed. It is not a format for parental directing.
- The family meeting is not an opportunity for kid-bashing; discipline should almost always happen somewhere else, where a child's feelings can be respected. The family meeting should be a positive experience for all family members.
- Family decisions and solutions should be arrived at by consensus, not majority vote, which would only serve to accentuate family divisions. Consensus means there *is* no decision until one is reached that all can live with, so an item will remain on the agenda until consensus is reached. This means that some items are discussed for weeks or months until everyone can agree. Of course, some items are not appropriate for agreement by consensus, such as where the family should live. However, if a job transfer requires a move, family members can discuss how to make the move as pleasant as possible.
- It is important to rotate the jobs that keep orderly family meetings functioning:
  - Chairperson—you may have an actual gavel that this person uses to call the meeting to order
  - Note-taker, Secretary, or Recorder—use a special pen or pencil or notepad for this position. See Jane Nelsen's website to download a Family Meeting Album (http://store.positivediscipline.com/Family-Meeting-Album_p_72.html)
  - Celebration Director—the family could create a list of ideas for family fun and dessert ideas at one of your first meetings, adding to it as needed. Fresh fruit or just-popped popcorn are sure hits in most families, so the ideas don't have to be costly or extravagant.

- Sometimes we hear from single parents that family meetings have been especially helpful in working through transitions and challenges without manipulation of any family member. Some stepfamilies have remarked that when they had family meetings, the children weren't as apt to pick up the labels "his/hers, mine, and ours" because everyone worked together to create the new family. The challenges they faced together pulled everyone in the same, rather than opposite, directions. All families, regardless of composition, have up and down situations that challenge family communication patterns.

- The family meeting is not an abdication of parental responsibility. Providing a forum through which children can be listened to, considered, and affirmed does not mean that *every* idea they have is open to a family vote. The responsible Christian family is the family that has aligned itself with basic principles, such as respectfulness, honesty, courtesy, and truthfulness. Further, the responsible Christian family has made rules of conduct regarding curfews, television viewing, homework, household chores, etc. The family meeting may well provide a forum for the discussion of these items, but just as responsibility ultimately lies with the parents, the final decision-making must lie there as well. An effective family meeting is one in which all family members know what is open for debate and what is not. Parents can ensure that the items not open for debate are limited to those that represent the basic family values and the rules that support them.

Concluding Thoughts

Time for a true confession. Remember "Marjorie" at the beginning of the chapter? Well, her name is really Mary, one of the authors. Although Mary was disillusioned when her children called the family meetings "Mom's meetings," she didn't quit—and neither did her family. Although their meetings were never textbook quality, they found that this family time was far more valuable than it may have sometimes appeared at the time.

One day, after leaving home for college her second year away from home, "Melanie" (really Wendy, Mary's daughter) called right after church, about the time the family had always had their family meeting. She asked, "You and Dad and Eric are having a family meeting, right?" Mary said, "No, we aren't meeting until 7 p.m. tonight because Eric is busy right after church. He isn't even home."

"Okay, then," Wendy replied, "I'll just have to call back. I have to hear from each of you what you think my options are in this situation I'm facing with one of my instructors. I'll call Erin and get her opinion, and then I'll call you guys later. Bye."

How many college-age girls would call home to get everybody's thoughts about a difficult decision? Every family occasionally struggles with family meetings. But whether the children in your family are young, school-aged, or teenagers, it's never too late to start. In the long run, the struggles with family meetings are worth it—worth it because of the life skills you will teach, the family togetherness you will experience, and the family memories you will treasure. And worth it because of the spiritual strengthening you will all experience as you work together to make your family an encouraging, inspiring, respectful place for everyone in it.

DO'S AND DON'TS
FOR SUCCESSFUL FAMILY MEETINGS

DO:

1. Remember the long-range purpose: To develop perceptions of belonging, significance, and capability—and to teach valuable life skills such as communication skills, problem solving skills, thinking skills, accountability, and cooperation.

2. Post an agenda in a visible place and encourage family members to write problems on it—or anything that needs to be discussed by the family—as they occur.

3. Start with compliments so family members learn to look for and to verbalize positive things about each other.

4. Brainstorm for solutions to problems. Start with wild and crazy ideas (for fun) and end with practical ideas that are useful and respectful to all concerned. Then choose one suggestion (by consensus) and try it for a week.

5. Schedule a family fun activity for later in the week—and all sports and other activities (including a chauffeur schedule).

6. Keep family meetings short: 10 to 30 minutes is usually enough, depending on the ages of your children. End with a family fun activity, game, or dessert.

DON'T:

1. Use family meetings as a platform for lectures and parental control.

2. Allow children to dominate and control. (Mutual respect is the key.)

3. Skip weekly family meetings. (They should be the most important date on your calendar.)

4. Forget that mistakes are wonderful opportunities to learn.

5. Forget that a family meeting is a process that teaches valuable life skills—not an exercise in perfection. Learning the skills takes time. Even unsuccessful solutions provide an opportunity to go back and try again—always focusing on respect and solutions.

6. Expect children under the age of four to participate in the process. (If younger children are too distracting, wait until they are in bed.)

Chapter 12

Celebrating the Family

Peace be with you!   *Peace to this house.*
(John 20:19)   (Luke 10:5)

Rebecca arrived home from college after her first year away and announced to her family that she no longer believed it was important to go to church. "If I want to talk to God, I can do so wherever and whenever I want. I don't need a church to talk to God." Her parents, who had gone away to college themselves and knew a little about teenage rebellion, wisely refused to take the bait that Rebecca took pleasure in dangling before them. But they were not prepared for Rebecca's comment as they sat down together for dinner.

During her absence from home that past year, Rebecca's parents had gotten a bit careless in their own spiritual life and had fallen out of the habit of saying a blessing before their meal. When they started to eat their salads without saying a blessing, Rebecca was outraged, making it clear that she expected things to be as they were when she left. She even volunteered to say the prayer. And again, her wise parents said nothing except, "Thank you, Rebecca."

What Rebecca missed during her year away at college was the comfort of the familiar, the comfort of those connective rituals that provide a sense of familiarity and security in life. Rebecca may not have said a blessing before meals in her dorm, but once she returned home she expected those rituals to be in place, just as they always had been.

We have explored the idea of using routines as a teaching and discipline tool, but routines also provide the comfort of the familiar, the framework within which we can grow and develop. In this chapter we will look at some of the rituals, traditions, and celebrations that healthy Christian families can establish in their lives to nurture stability, peace, and joy in their homes. We will look at ways Christian parents can stay tuned in to their child's school experience. Finally, we will look at the various ways our Christian faith provides opportunities for us, as families, to interact with the larger community in service.

Rituals and Traditions

Rituals and traditions are routines that have achieved significance above and beyond their basic meaning. Cleaning the backyard on Saturday morning is a routine; going out to breakfast or lunch as a family after church on Sunday is a ritual. Rituals and traditions are routines that have been blessed.

Rituals and traditions refer to all those familiar celebrations and activities (birthday parties and unique celebrations, special holiday traditions, going out to breakfast after church on Sunday, going out to dinner after the first day of school, story time and prayer at the end of the day, special ways of celebrating Christmas, etc.) that become part of a family's identity. These rituals are often taken for granted—until someone forgets to do them, that is. These are the moments that each of us remembers for a lifetime, the special shared times that become cherished memories. We will explore several family rituals and traditions in this chapter. But first we need to look at why celebrating your family is so important.

A Socially Toxic Environment

Dr. James Garbarino of Cornell University has written extensively of what he calls our "socially toxic environment." Garbarino describes all those factors—from media images of violence and irresponsible sexuality to the allure of materialism and its attendant social pressures—that confront today's young people. Most parents know intuitively to protect their children from physically toxic situations, like watching out for cars when crossing the street, not running with scissors, or wearing a seat belt. But many are unprepared to protect their children from situations that are toxic to their Christian faith and to their healthy cognitive, emotional, and social development.

The family is the most important force in society for dealing with, teaching about, and protecting our children from those socially toxic factors. Church, school, and community and governmental agencies are critical in providing support, but the family is the key to giving children the tools they will need for dealing with the world "out there." How will you respond to this challenge and still create a home that is loving and happy?

What about School?

Few parents stop to question the value of education, especially in this era of rapidly-accelerating technology. Parents want happiness and success for their children, and education is a valuable way to achieve those goals. For Christian parents, however, school poses some problems. You are obviously reading this book because you care about creating a Christian home; you want your children to grow in faith and wisdom as well as in skills and abilities. Most parents at some time stop to consider the options: should their child attend public school or a faith-based school? Should they be home schooled? What are the drawbacks and benefits of each choice?

> *...it is critically important that you stay tuned into your child's education, and that you carefully consider what your child is learning— her attitudes and values, as well as her ABCs.*

A comprehensive discussion of the comparative merits of public and private education, as well as home schooling, is beyond the scope of this book. Each can have tremendous benefits that can be compared by each individual family. You can and should investigate the options in your own community. Whichever one you choose, it is critically important that you stay tuned into your child's education, and that you carefully consider what your child is learning—her attitudes and values, as well as her ABCs.

Here are some suggestions for coping with schools (regardless of the type your child attends), and for making sure that what your child experiences at school supports the values you teach at home:

- **Be involved.** There is no better way to support your child than to be a part of her education. Attend parent-teacher conferences and back-to-school nights; volunteer to help in your child's classroom. If work makes this impossible, call your child's teacher from time to time just to check in. Children benefit in wonderful ways when parents and teachers can work together.
- **Listen.** Be sure you take time to really listen when your child talks about school (not as easy as it sounds for busy parents). Listen when he talks about friends, playground behavior, classroom discipline, and privileges he enjoys. When you hear stories or ideas that clash with your own values or that worry you, take time to do some teaching;

ask "what" and "how" questions, and invite your child to think about what is happening. Many schools still rely heavily on punishment and rewards, approaches that have been shown to be ineffective in changing behavior over the long term and that are discouraging to children. You may want to volunteer to start a parents' group at your school, or to share Positive Discipline with your child's teacher. (We highly recommend *Positive Discipline in the Classroom, Revised 2nd Edition*, Nelsen, Prima, 2000 and *Parenting through the School Years . . . and Beyond!* by Mike Brock, available at on-line bookstores or through the author.

- **Beware of the homework wars.** Schoolwork is a child's responsibility. Still, many parents tell horror stories of hours spent each day coaxing, wheedling, and begging children to do their homework. If schoolwork is a problem in your home, you might want to put it on the agenda for a family meeting and invite children to help you brainstorm for solutions. You can also suggest that your child and his teacher work out a plan together. You can suggest and remind, but doing work *for* children, or standing over their shoulders "making" them do it will destroy much of the peace and joy you've worked so hard to create in your home.

- **Encourage the joy of learning.** You can make learning a part of your family time, and you can model by your own behavior that education is important. Create a comfortable space for children to work and learn in. Be sure they have adequate time to read and study (as well as to relax). Reading out loud together teaches young children language skills and is one of the best ways to encourage school readiness; it can also be an enjoyable part of your family time, especially when children are able to read to you.

Clearly there is much for the Christian parent to consider when approaching the subject of schooling. Take time to clarify your values, check out the various alternatives available, and make the effort to understand the needs of your child. Weigh carefully whether or not the school meets the various needs—academic, social, emotional, physical, and spiritual—of your child and family.

> Weigh carefully whether or not the school meets the various needs—academic, social, emotional, physical, and spiritual—of your child and family.

Education can be a reason for celebration, too. Make every effort to ensure that your children's educational experiences are joyous and, indeed, cause for celebration. Rituals and traditions can add to the joy that your family experiences. Celebrate the beginning of the year and the end of the year, pausing to recognize that your child has reached another transition in life. Make report card time an opportunity to celebrate, regardless of what the report card looks like (remember to look for the positive). Some families go out to dinner to celebrate their children's achievements and proud moments. Make parent/teacher conferences an opportunity for "good finding," and celebrate those days as well. Look for every opportunity you can to mark the events associated with your children's schooling and they will learn to see schooling as both a positive experience and an extension of their normal family activities.

The Christian Family as Oasis

A Christian family serves as an oasis, a safe place in which children can experience unconditional love, acceptance, affirmation, positive role modeling, and kind, firm, consistent discipline. It is also, as we have learned, a place where they can make—and learn from—mistakes. The world out there will not always provide these things. Indeed, as Garbarino suggests, it is doing an increasingly poor job of supporting the efforts of families to provide them. Rituals and traditions help create those safe places and moments of belonging in which we can communicate our values and demonstrate our love for one another.

One of the Positive Discipline tools available to parents is the limiting of words you use and letting the routine be the boss. This is also true for rituals and traditions. Rituals such as saying the blessing before meals, saying prayers at the end of the day, volunteering at the church food pantry, or visiting Grandma after church on Sunday all teach important lessons effectively without the need for preaching or lecturing.

Sometimes, in their efforts to teach an important value, parents spend too much energy talking about it instead of just doing it. Actions usually do speak much louder than words alone. The family that offers service to the community on a regular basis is learning more about giving than the family where Dad or Mom merely offers weekly sermons on the subject.

> *If character and values are important to you, be sure you live them each day.*

If character and values are important to you, be sure you *live* them each day. You may also be able to begin family traditions that reinforce what you teach and believe, from adopting a park to clean up to serving Thanksgiving dinner at a homeless shelter.

The Family Dinner

James Michener, perhaps America's greatest storyteller, wrote in *This Noble Land* (Random House Value Publishing, 1999) that at the top of his list of "essential components in the education of a child" is "living in a family that has an orderly dinner every night at which there is lively discussion of important topics." In *Parenting through the School Years . . . and Beyond!* (formerly *Seven Strategies for Developing Capable Students*) author Mike Brock examines several studies that positively correlate success in school with living in a family that eats dinner together on a regular basis.

What is it about eating dinner together that correlates with success in school and in life? Are people who eat dinner together smarter than those who don't? Probably not. Perhaps families who take the time to eat together create an environment that is connected, stable, and peaceful, one where children have regular opportunities to talk with parents, listen to siblings, and most important, experience a sense of belonging and significance.

Gathering around the table to eat dinner together is a simple prescription for the renewal of family life, so simple we are tempted to minimize its importance. But it would be a serious mistake to do so. Consider taking an hour, if possible, for dinner with your family. Avoid the temptation to run from the table as soon as the dishes are cleared. Take time to re-think dinner with your family and ditch *any* form of technology during that special family time. Here are five recent research studies to convince you:

- Family dinners are more important than play, story time and other family events in the development of vocabulary of younger children. (Harvard Research, 1996)
- Frequent family meals are associated with a lower risk of smoking, drinking and using drugs; with a lower incidence of depressive symptoms and suicidal thoughts; and with better grades in 11 to 18 year olds. (Archives of Pediatrics and Adolescent Medicine, 2004)
- Adolescent girls who have frequent family meals, and a positive atmosphere during those meals, are less likely to have eating disorders. (University of Minnesota, 2004)
- Kids who eat most often with their parents are 40% more likely to get mainly A's and B's in school than kids who have two or fewer family dinners a week. (National Center on Addiction and Substance Abuse at Columbia University)
- Take time to read this 2006 article, "The Magic of the Family Meal," if you still aren't sold on the benefits of eating together as a family: http://www.time.com/time/magazine/article/0,9171,1200760,00.html

For some families, eating dinner together every night just isn't possible because of work schedules, soccer practices, or evening meetings. You can still decide on at least one or two nights a week that you will keep free from outside distractions and make them special dinner times. If you can only manage dinner together once a week, make an effort to create a real celebration. Make it a more formal setting, perhaps adding a candle and soft music. The children in one family took turns writing encouraging notes with Scriptures or cheerful messages to place by each person's plate. This special time can provide priceless opportunities for connection and celebration in your family.

You can communicate to your family that they are more important than television, more important than outside schedules, and more important than the person on the other end of the cell phone. Of course, as children grow up and peers become a larger and larger part of their world, they may not want to linger at the table as long as parents would like. This provides a great opportunity for respectful problem-solving.

In the Peterson family, Dad became upset when everyone wanted to leave the table before he was through eating. He complained about this for several months before he remembered to put the problem on the family meeting agenda. When the problem came up for discussion at the next meeting, Mom and the two teenagers complained that he ate too slowly, and that it was boring to just sit there and watch him. Dad finally shared that he felt his family didn't love him when they left him sitting at the table all alone. Mom and the kids were very surprised to hear this and tried to reassure Dad that of course they loved him, but that it was hard to just sit at the table after they were finished eating. During the brainstorming several suggestions were made:

1) Dad could eat faster.
2) Everyone else could eat slower.
3) They could sit with Dad for ten minutes after they were done just to show him they loved him.
4) Instead of being bored they could each take turns telling about their favorite part of the day, share their goals for the week, or plan what they would like to do for fun as a family.

The whole family was able to agree to both suggestions three and four. The discussion also led to greater understanding of each other and of their different styles. They realized that it would stress Dad out to eat faster, and that it wouldn't hurt the rest of them to slow down a bit. They especially realized how important it was to express their love and caring for each other.

However you are able to work it out in your family, nothing will provide a safer and more secure harbor for children, including teenagers, than experiencing and remembering how important it was for the whole family to spend time breaking bread together.

The Influence of Family Life on the Child

The dinner table may be the perfect metaphor for the renewal of family life. Many "experts" have spoken about the death of the American family. The statistics are chilling: So many fatherless homes, so many unwed pregnant teenagers, so many cases of spousal abuse and child abuse, so many teenage suicides, and on and on. It is a dismal picture. The American family is dead, these experts declare, and we need to provide other models to replace it; the churches, community organizations, and the local, state, and federal governments must step up to the plate and offer themselves as alternatives to the now-deceased American family.

Although we do not share this pessimism, we agree that schools, churches, community organizations, and government could do more to support families. But they are not and never will be *alternatives* to the family.

Just how important is the influence of the family on the child? All of the Positive Discipline books have explored Alfred Adler's theories on birth order and the effects it has on a child's perception of his role in the family. We believe (as discussed more thoroughly in Chapter 5) that how a child perceives himself in relationship to his family exerts more influence on him than any other system, organization, institution, or even experience that he might have in life. As the world becomes more and more hectic and fast-paced, more and more confusing and technologically overpowering, more and more threatening and socially toxic, the influence of the family becomes critical. When all else is confusing and confounding, the family remains the one constant that can be counted on—sitting around the table eating dinner together, sharing the experiences of the day, listening to each others' joys and frustrations, and celebrating each other's lives.

> ...there is something extra special about taking time to spend with each child individually.

It seems easy enough to see the influence of family life on young children. Sometimes, though, we overlook the importance of these early years on the choices grown children make when establishing traditions of their own. Mary's grown children still look forward to the traditional early-morning chorus of "Happy Birthday" that they've heard since they were children—even though now the singing may happen over the telephone. One year, when one of the children was away at college, the "Happy Birthday" chorus was saved on an answering machine to replay during moments of homesickness. Moments like these create deposits in our emotional bank accounts that sustain us during times of stress and separation.

Family Night

Dad's job forces him to be out of town four nights a week, Monday through Thursday. Mom has part-time work outside the home, a full carpool schedule before and after, and the cooking to do at the end of the day. (The other family chores are divided as equally as possible among all family members) Friday night is reserved for Mom and Dad to spend together, and on Saturday nights the kids plan activities with their friends. Sunday is reserved as the night the family eats together. It is also reserved as "family night."

For many families, family night is an extension of the family meal. Family night simply means one night set aside each week for the family to be together. You may have a family meeting, play games, tell stories, read to each other, make dessert together, do projects, plan outings and vacations, and so on. Like the family meal, family night is simply one more opportunity to communicate to children that they are worthy of our time and attention, that they are more important than all the distractions that the world places before us.

Family nights can be enhanced by allowing the children to choose the activity, by ensuring some variation in the activities, and by throwing in surprises from time to time (a trip to an ice cream shop, for example). The key is to schedule it and stick with it, like the family meal. And when the teenagers start drifting away, keep on doing it anyway—they will drift back, and when they do they will appreciate the oasis you have continued to provide on family night.

One final note: Don't forget one-on-one time with the children. As positive an experience as it is to have the entire family together, there is something extra special about taking time to spend with each child individually. Children have the opportunity to feel a special sense of belonging and worth when Mom or Dad seeks them out for some time together. Special time is a powerful communicator of significance, one worth making the time for.

Closing Time

How many children have ended their day with the simple prayer, "Now I lay me down to sleep, I pray the Lord my soul to keep"? No matter how hectic the day might be and no matter how many negative experiences may have occurred, ending that day on a peaceful and positive note can go a long way toward creating stability and comfort. We cannot guarantee that our children's days will be filled with positive experiences, nor should we even try, but we can make a concerted effort to end the day in a reassuring and supportive manner.

If our children can go to bed at peace about the day they have just completed, then they will be more likely to feel optimistic about the day to come. Send them to bed angry and alienated, and they will learn to anticipate (and give back) more of the same.

For that reason, many families have a designated "closing time," after which no more individual work is done and all family members can enjoy each other's company before it's time to turn out the lights and go to bed. Even if this only happens for fifteen minutes, and even if Mom and Dad still have more to do before the evening is over, setting aside this time for the children to be together with the parents can be a very pleasant way to end their day.

At closing time, all homework, housework, and office work stops. The family comes together to end the day with personal reflections, a story, a prayer, and/or a Scriptural reading. One of the most heartwarming experiences for co-author Jane Nelsen is to visit her son's family and participate in their evening ritual of reading a Scripture (the four children take turns) and then kneeling together for family prayer. The feeling of completeness in love for God and family is magnificent and peaceful.

Closing time helps to refocus the family, to remind all family members that whatever has happened in each one's day, whatever directions each family member has taken, they can now come together as a family to share some time together. What a pleasant way to end the day, one certain to provide a more peaceful night's sleep.

The Power of Touch

There was a time several years ago when Mike had been emotionally absent from his family. His son, Thomas, about twelve at the time, approached him, and with the simplicity and honesty that is found only in children said, "Dad, you haven't hardly even touched me all day!" And he was right. Thomas had learned that Mike's introspective and somewhat quiet nature was "just the way Dad is." But the fact that not once during the day had Dad hugged him, patted his shoulder, or even poked him playfully on the arm was more than he could handle. "You have hardly even touched me all day." What a powerful indictment!

As we discovered in Chapter 10, communication is only about twenty percent verbal. The remaining eighty percent of our message is contained in our body language, tone of voice, posture, attitude, and so on. Touch is a powerful communicator. Have we not all experienced the hug, pat, kiss, or warm handshake that communicated a message far better than words?

It is sad that physical touch has become such a sensitive issue today because of abuse problems. Teachers are routinely instructed by administrators to avoid touching a student lest that touch be misconstrued, resulting in embarrassment, discomfort, confrontation, lawsuits, or worse. Some parents also hold back when it comes to physical touch, often because it is the approach they were raised with and are most comfortable with even in their own home.

There are at least half a dozen Scriptures that encourage Christians to "greet one another with a holy kiss." We do not need to be reminded that abuses do occur and must be guarded against; touch must always be appropriate, and children do need to be taught how to resist hurtful touches. But when our vigilance in preventing abuse leads us to avoid affectionate, reassuring touch, we are contributing to another form of abuse, the abuse of emotional detachment.

We have all read reports of the critical need for physical touch in newborns, how picking up a child, holding him close, and stroking his face can be critical to his very survival. People who work in nursing homes tell us that physical touch can make a difference in the quality of life of the elderly, even prolonging their lives. Men and women throughout the world regularly shake hands, embrace, or kiss each other in their daily greeting. We all need physical touch, and we need it regularly.

Emotional stability in the home is strengthened when family members touch each other affectionately. In addition to making contact, providing closeness, and showing affection, loving physical touch helps children understand the difference between touch that is appropriate and that which isn't. Spouses can model appropriate physical touch by their own natural expressions of it to each other, as well as to their children (research tells us that children have healthier relationships when they have witnessed appropriate physical affection between their parents). Our children will have plenty of opportunities from television, the movies, and the internet to learn how hugs and kisses can be abused; they need to learn from us that they are natural signs of affection that happy, healthy, emotionally secure Christian adults can express without fear.

> *...when our vigilance in preventing abuse leads us to avoid affectionate, reassuring touch, we are contributing to another form of abuse, the abuse of emotional detachment.*

It is truly unfortunate that, as reported by a Gallup poll some years ago, about half of American parents believe it is "sometimes necessary to discipline a child with a good, hard spanking." This is a sad commentary on the state of parenting and parent education, and it presents a challenge for all of us who would strive for a more respectful way of guiding our children. Let's ensure that the physical contact we have with our children is always loving, soothing, and comforting, and a source of blessing rather than pain.

Making the Lord's Day Special

One of the earliest commandments was to "Remember the Sabbath day by keeping it holy." (Exodus 20: 8) Many of us cherish memories of going out to eat as a family after Sunday service, or coming home to the aroma of a pot roast meal that is cooked only on Sundays. For others, the memory may be of a trip to Grandma's house or a regular get-together with friends. These can all become rituals in their own right, but when we make them part of our Sunday worship, we raise them to a new level of meaning in our lives. Not only do they serve as connective rituals for the family, they help create a warm feeling for attendance at Sunday services.

Let's be honest about it: Parents weren't always excited about going to Sunday services when they were children (and sometimes may not be excited about it even as adults). But when Sunday services also means going out to eat as a family or going to Grandma's house, the picture changes. It becomes not just a duty but a celebration—a connective ritual that celebrates the family.

For many families, Sunday is also the ideal time for family dinners, family meetings, and family nights. Celebrating Sunday with activities such as these serves both to reinforce the importance of the Lord's Day as well as provide a serene time within which families can enjoy simply being together. The Lord's Day has lost much of its cultural support over the years, and that's regrettable. Christian families can decide to be proactive and make of that day a special occasion for celebration and togetherness. In our increasingly busy world, that one day set aside for each other is truly appreciated!

A Place Where You Want to Be

What all this adds up to—making the Lord's Day special, family dinners, family meetings, family nights, and physical signs of affection—is a home in which children feel welcome and comfortable. Take a moment to ask yourself this question: Is your home a place where your children *want* to be?

When choices arise between staying home with the family and engaging in unhealthy activities, will they choose, instead, to stay home? Will they be comfortable inviting their friends over? Making sure that the home is a comfortable place to be—a place of encouragement, support, and affirmation; a place where each person is loved unconditionally; a place free from constant nagging and criticism (remember Ephesians 6:4-6 NKJV: "Fathers, do not provoke your children.")—will help you answer those questions in the affirmative, providing the safe refuge that your children need and deserve.

Sharing the Blessings

We began this chapter with the story of Rebecca, who returned home from college with ideas of her own about the importance of going to church on Sunday. Rebecca was letting her parents know that she was becoming her own person and, typically, chose an issue that was important to her parents to make her point. But Rebecca's parents had made the effort through the years to create and celebrate positive rituals and traditions and, in spite of herself, Rebecca learned to appreciate and value those rituals and traditions. In the end, those traditions and the love and belonging her family nurtured would bring her back to church on Sunday, a habit she now has incorporated into her own growing family.

We celebrate the family when we create opportunities to connect with each other on a regular basis and then share with others—through outreach, participation in neighborhood activities, community service, and church attendance—what we have learned within the oasis of the Christian family. Positive Discipline can help by providing many of the tools for creating a healthy family, one in which our children can learn the characteristics and life skills that will serve them so well in later life. The teachings of Jesus and the tools for developing healthy, respectful, loving families—that is surely a combination worth celebrating!

"But, as for me and my household, we will serve the Lord." (Joshua 24:15)

About the Authors

Mary Hughes, MHR, Certified Positive Discipline Lead Trainer, is the mother of three adult children, grandmother of four, and great-grandmother of one. Mary has taught parenting, early childhood education, and family relationship-strengthening for over forty years in a variety of settings. She and her husband, Gary, lead the Marriage and Family Care ministries in her home church in Bellevue, Nebraska, and teach parenting on a regular basis.

Mike Brock, LPC, dad of two adult children, is a Dallas-area licensed professional counselor, spiritual director, and seminar leader. In addition to *Positive Discipline in the Christian Home,* he is the author of *Be Still and Know that I Am God: Reflections on God, Connection, and the Gift of Presence* and *Parenting through the School Years . . . and Beyond!*

Dr. Jane Nelsen, EdD, MFT, mother of seven children and grandmother of twenty-one, is a licensed Marriage and Family Therapist and author or co-author of eighteen books including the *Positive Discipline* series, *Raising Self-Reliant Children in a Self-Indulgent World,* and *Serenity,* as well as several training manuals, CD and DVD programs. When not traveling to present workshops, she travels between California and Utah to spend time with her husband, Barry, and her many children and grandchildren.

FOR MORE INFORMATION

The authors are available for lectures, workshops, and seminars for parents, parenting educators, therapists, psychologists, social workers, nurses, counselors, school administrators, teachers, churches and corporations. (These can be tailored to fit your needs.)

Mary Hughes, MHR
enrich3726@cox.net
www.enrich-abilities.com

Mike Brock, LPC
mike@mikebrock.org
www.mikebrock.org

Jane Nelsen, EdD, LMFT
jane@positivediscipline.com
www.positivediscipline.com

The Positive Discipline Association promotes and encourages the development of respectful relationships in families, schools, businesses and community systems, including communities of faith. This non-profit corporation provides training, training materials and follow-up services, as well as advanced certification and support for the trainers. Adlerian/ Dreikursian principles are foundational in every area of training.

For more information or to be trained to deliver Positive Discipline workshops, go to www.positivediscipline.org/ or contact:

Positive Discipline Association
9417 Remuda Path, San Antonio, TX 78254
PDA Office: 866.POS.DISC (866.767.3472)
PDA Office email: posdis@satx.rr.com

Index